对照

"读"有所得

天使与魔鬼
An gels and Demons

主　编　关晓薇　高　鹏
副主编　陶　源　王　倩　周晓霞
编　委　韩　芳　张力升

大连理工大学出版社
DALIAN UNIVERSITY OF TECHNOLOGY PRESS

图书在版编目（CIP）数据

天使与魔鬼：汉英对照 / 关晓薇, 高鹏主编. --
大连：大连理工大学出版社，2012.7
（"读"有所得）
ISBN 978-7-5611-7063-2

Ⅰ.①天… Ⅱ.①关… ②高… Ⅲ.①汉语－英语－
对照读物②散文集－中国－现代 Ⅳ.①H319.4：Ⅰ

中国版本图书馆CIP数据核字(2012)第144016号

大连理工大学出版社出版
地址:大连市软件园路80号　　邮政编码：116023
发行：0411-84708842　邮购：0411-84703636　传真：0411-84701466
E-mail:dutp@dutp.cn　　URL: http://www.dutp.cn
辽宁星海彩色印刷有限公司印刷　　　大连理工大学出版社发行

幅面尺寸：168mm×235mm　　　印张：12.25　　　字数：185千字
印数：1~6000
2012年7月第1版　　　　　　　　　　2012年7月第1次印刷

责任编辑：张婵云　　　　　　　　　　　　　　责任校对：孙佳
装帧设计：对岸书影

ISBN 978-7-5611-7063-2　　　　　　　　　定价：22.00元

前 言 preface

　　我们生活在同一个世界，然而每个人的世界又是那么不同。这种不同来源于我们是选择倾听天使的声音，还是选择魔鬼陪伴左右。奉献、勇气、宽容、信心与执着的天使让生命充满阳光；嫉妒、悲观、胆怯、自私和虚荣的魔鬼使生活变得黑暗。

　　"让你的世界从此不同"，这正是我们编写此套中英双语读本的目的。本系列共分两册：《天使与魔鬼》和《植物与僵尸》。本册书：《天使与魔鬼》，精选了50篇富含人生哲理的短文，讲述的是五个天使的神奇和五个魔鬼的丑陋，从不同角度启发我们如何正确选择积极的人生态度和生活方式。从天使身上，你可以读到从人性里渗透出的各种光芒。让我们的故事给在成长中身处困境和迷惘中的你以最大的鼓舞和最深切的共鸣。

　　人是善变的动物，时而为纯善天使，时而为枯恶魔头，遗憾的是人无法区分也不会控制自己的情绪。所以，弱者任思绪控制行为，强者让行为控制思绪。"在成功的路上，最大的敌人其实并不是缺少机会，或是资历浅薄，成功的最大敌人是缺乏对自己情绪的控制。愤怒时，不能制怒，使周围的合作者望而却步；消沉时，放纵自己的萎靡，把许多稍纵即逝的机会白白浪费。"

　　我们希望你在赏析美文的同时，提升英文阅读能力；盼望你能思索各色品质的意义，感受生活的魅力与智慧，让你的心灵获得滋养，领悟人生的真谛，在各种历练中慢慢成长。期待你活出不一样的人生！

编者

2012.6

目　录

天使篇

1

魔鬼篇

奉献天使

勇气天使

宽容天使

信心天使

天使篇

执着天使

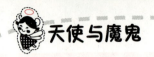

奉献天使篇
[之一]

A Boy and His Tree

> Old tree roots are the best place to lean on and rest. Come here, please sit down with me and have a rest.
>
> 老树墩就是倚着休息的最好地方。过来，和我一起坐下休息吧。

A long time ago, there was a huge apple tree. A little boy loved to come and play around it every day. He climbed to the tree top, ate the apples, took a nap (小睡) under the shadow… He loved the tree and the tree loved to play with him.

Time went by… The little boy had grown up and he no longer played around the tree.

One day, the boy came back to the tree and looked sad. "Come and play with me," the tree asked the boy.

"I am no longer a kid. I don't play around trees anymore," the boy replied, "I want toys. I need money to buy them." "Sorry, but I don't have money… But you can pick all my apples and sell them. So you will have money." The boy was so excited. He picked all the apples on the tree and left happily. The boy didn't come back after he picked the apples. The tree was sad.

One day, the boy returned and the tree was so excited. "Come and play with me," the tree said. "I don't have time to play. I have to work for my family. We need a house for shelter. Can you help me?" "Sorry, but I don't have a house. But you can cut off my branches to build your house." So the boy cut all the branches of the tree and left happily.

The tree was glad to see him happy but the boy didn't appear since then. The tree was again lonely and sad. One hot summer day, the boy returned and the tree was delighted. "Come and play with me!" the tree said.

"I am sad and getting old. I want to go sailing to relax myself. Can you give me a boat?" "Use my trunk (树干) to build the boat. You can sail and be happy." So the boy cut the tree trunk to make a boat. He went sailing and did not show up for a long time.

Finally, the boy returned after he left for so many years. "Sorry, my boy. But I don't have anything for you anymore. No more apples for you," the tree said. "I don't have teeth to bite," the boy replied. "No more trunk for you to climb on." "I am too old for that now," the boy said. "I really want to give you something… The only thing left is my dying roots," the tree said with tears. "I don't need much now, just a place to rest. I am tired after all these years," the boy replied. "Good! Old tree roots are the best place to lean on and rest. Come here, please sit down with me and have a rest." The boy sat down and the tree was glad and smiled with tears…

This is a story of everyone. The tree is our parent. When we were young, we loved to play with Mom and Dad… When we grow up, we leave them, and only come to them when we need something or when we are in trouble. No matter what, parents will always be there and give everything they could to make you happy. You may think that the boy is cruel to the tree but that's how all of us are treating our parents. (559 words)

(Extracted from "http://www.ebigear.com/news-196-77416.html")

孩子和树

很久以前，有一棵高大的苹果树。一个小男孩每天都喜欢来到树旁玩耍。他爬到树顶，吃苹果，在树荫里打盹……他爱这棵树，树也爱和他一起玩。

随着时间的流逝……小男孩长大了，他不再到树旁玩耍了。

一天，男孩回到树旁，看起来很悲伤。"来和我玩吧，"树说。

"我不再是小孩了，我不会再到树下玩耍了，"男孩答道，"我想要玩具，我需要钱来买。""很遗憾，我没有钱……但是你可以采摘我所有的苹果拿去卖。这样你就有钱了。"男孩很兴奋，他摘掉树上所有的苹果，然后高兴地离开了。自从那以后男孩没有回来，树很伤心。

一天，男孩回来了，树非常兴奋。"来和我玩吧，"树说。"我没有时间玩，我得为我的家庭工作。我们需要一个房子来遮风挡雨，你能帮我吗？""很遗憾，我没有房子。但是你可以砍下我的树枝来建房。"于是男孩砍下所有的树枝，高高兴兴地离开了。

看到他高兴，树也很高兴。但是，自从那以后男孩再没出现，树又孤独伤心起来。在一个炎热的夏日，男孩回到树旁，树很高兴。"来和我玩吧！"树说。

"我很伤心，我开始老了。我想去航海放松自己。你能不能给我一条船？""用我的树干去造一条船。你就能航海了，你会高兴的。"于是，男孩砍倒树干去造船。他扬帆远航，很长一段时间未露面。

许多年后男孩终于回来了。"很遗憾，我的孩子。我再也没有任何东西可以给你了。没有苹果给你，"树说。"我没有牙齿啃，"男孩回答。"没有树干供你爬。""现在我老了，爬不上去了，"男孩说。"我真的想把一切都给你……我唯一剩下的东西是快要死去的树墩，"树含着眼泪说。"现在，我不需要什么东西，只需要一个地方来休息。经过了这些年我太累了，"男孩回答。"太好了！老树墩就是倚着休息的最好地方。过来，和我一起坐下休息吧。"男孩坐下了，树很高兴，含泪而笑……

这是一个发生在每个人身上的故事。那棵树就像我们的父母。我们小的时候，喜欢和爸爸妈妈玩……长大后，便离开他们，只有在我们需要父母，或是遇到了困难的时候，才会回去找他们。尽管如此，父母却总是有求必应，为了我们的幸福，无私地奉献自己的一切。你也许觉得那个男孩对待树很残忍，但我们何尝不是这样呢？

父母如同那棵树，保护我们成长，他们无私地奉献着自己，让孩子在成长中得到保护。他们的付出不要任何回报，他们为儿女的成长感到欣慰，却无悔于自己的付出。

"老树墩就是倚着休息的最好地方。过来，和我一起坐下休息吧。"当父母步入老年，他们所需要的是陪伴着他们，和他们一起聊聊天。

父母是我们心灵的港湾，用他们无私的爱丰富着我们的成长过程，我们多陪陪爸爸妈妈，用爱温暖他们的心，如天使一样给予他们一点点心灵的陪伴和精神上的安慰。

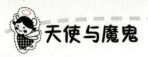

天使与魔鬼

奉献天使篇

[之二]

A Good-bye Kiss

> I wish I had been a man then. If I had been a man, I would never have told my Dad I was too old for a goodbye kiss.
>
> 我真希望那时候我是一个真正的男子汉。如果我是个男子汉的话，我绝不会告诉爸爸我已经长大，不适合吻别了。

Once my friend Frank told us of his childhood, "My Dad was a fisherman who loved the sea. He had his own boat, but it was hard making a living on the sea. He worked hard and would stay out until he caught enough to feed the family."

"My father was a big man, and he was strong from pulling the nets and fighting the sea. When you got close to him, he smelled like the ocean. He would wear his old canvas(帆布) and foul(糟糕的) –weather coat. His rain hat would be pulled down over his brow. No matter how much my mother washed them, they would still smell of the sea and of fish."

"When the weather was bad he would drive me to school. He had this old truck that he used in his fishing business. That truck was older than he was. It would wheeze (喘息) and rattle (格格响) down the road. You could hear it coming for blocks. As he would drive toward the school, I would shrink down into the seat hoping to disappear. He would pull right up in front, and it seemed like everybody would be standing around and watching. Then he would lean over and give me a big kiss on the cheek and tell me to be a good boy. It was so embarrassing for me. Here, I was twelve years old, and my Dad would lean over and kiss me goodbye!"

"I remember the day I decided I was too old for a goodbye kiss. When

6

we got to the school and came to a stop, he had his usual big smile. He started to lean toward me, but I put my hand up and said, 'No, Dad.' It was the first time I had ever talked to him that way, and he had this surprised look on his face. I said, 'Dad, I'm too old for a goodbye kiss.'

My Dad looked at me for the longest time and turned and looked out the windshield. 'You're right. You are a big boy...a man. I won't kiss you anymore.'"

Tears began to well up in Frank's eyes, as he spoke. "It wasn't long after that when my Dad went to sea and never came back. It was a day when most of the fleet(舰队) stayed in, but not Dad. He had a big family to feed. He must have gotten into a gale and was trying to save the nets and the floats."

I looked at Frank and saw that tears were running down his cheeks. Frank spoke again, "You don't know what I would give to have my Dad give me just one more kiss on the cheek...to feel his rough old face...to smell the ocean on him...to feel his arm around my neck. I wish I had been a man then. If I had been a man, I would never have told my Dad I was too old for a goodbye kiss." (514 words)

吻别

有一次我的朋友弗兰克给我们讲了他童年的往事："我爸爸是位渔夫，他非常热爱大海。有一条自己的小船，但是靠在海上捕鱼为生太艰难了。他辛勤地劳动着，总是一直待在海上直到捕到足以养活全家的鱼为止。"

"我爸爸身材高大。由于长期拉网捕鱼，与大海搏斗的缘故，身体强壮。走进他时，你能够闻到他身上散发出来的大海的气息。他穿着旧的帆布衣服和在糟糕的天气里穿的衣服。不管妈妈怎么洗他的衣服，总是有一股大海和鱼的味道。"

"天气不好的时候，爸爸会开自己卖鱼时用的旧卡车送我去学校。那辆卡车比他的年龄还大，一路上不停格格地喘息前进，离着几个街区以外都能听见。车快开到学校的时候，我都缩在座位上，希望自己消失。他每次都把车停在学校正门口，好像每个人都站在一旁观看。然后，他弯下身子在我脸上重重地亲了一口，告诉我要做一个好孩子。这让我觉得很难堪。那时我都12岁了，而爸爸还俯身和我吻别！"

"我还记得有一天，我认为自己已经长大，不再合适吻别了。我们到了学校停下来的时候，爸爸像往常一样露出了灿烂的笑容，他开始向我俯下身来，但是我抬手挡住了他，'不，爸爸。'我第一次那样对他说话，他看上去很吃惊。我说，'爸爸，我已经长大了，不再适合吻别了。'"

爸爸盯着我看了好长时间，他转过身子，透过挡风玻璃向外望去。'没错，你已经是一个大男孩儿……一个男子汉了。我再也不这样亲吻你了。'"

讲到这儿，弗兰克泪水在眼眶里打转。"从那之后没多久，爸爸出海后就再也没回来了。那天大多数船只都留在海湾，除了爸爸。他要养活一大家子人，出海后卷入了旋风，那时候还试着把网和浮子捞回来。"

我看着弗兰克，眼泪顺着他的脸颊流下来。弗兰克又开口了，"你们不知道，如果我爸爸能再亲我一下……让我感觉一下他那粗糙、苍老的面孔……闻一闻他身上海洋的气息……享受他搂着我脖子的感觉，那么我付出什么都愿意。我真希望那时候我是一个真正的男子汉。如果我是个男子汉的话，我绝不会告诉爸爸我已经长大，不适合吻别了。"

父爱是严肃的、刚强的、博大精深的，给予我们坚强、自信、宽容。父爱如山，山一样强健的体魄，给予我们无穷的力量，让我们偎依，使我们品味一份宽厚仁慈的真爱！

"我真希望那时候我是一个真正的男子汉。如果我是个男子汉的话，我绝不会告诉爸爸我已经长大，不适合吻别了。"多年以后，弗兰克才知道父亲的吻别有着多么重要的意义。父亲的一切，早已融进永不止息地送给他攀登的力量中了。

父亲用厚实的臂膀支撑着整个家庭，父亲用亲情温暖着孩子的心灵。让我们大声说出对父亲的爱，永恒地留在父亲的眼中和心里。父亲如奉献天使，把心中的祝福化作阳光般的温暖。

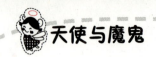

奉献天使篇
[之三]

The Window

The nurse responded that the man was blind and could not even see the wall. She said, "Perhaps he just wanted to encourage you."

护士回答说，那个人是盲人，甚至连墙都看不见。她说："也许他只是想鼓励你。"

Two men, both seriously ill, occupied(居住) the same hospital room. One man was allowed to sit up in his bed for an hour each afternoon to help drain the fluid from his lungs. His bed was next to the room's only window. The other man had to spend all his time flatting on his back.

The men talked for hours on end. They spoke of their wives and families, their homes, their jobs, their involvement in the military and a whole lot of things. Every afternoon when the man in the bed by the window could sit up, he would pass the time by describing to his roommate all the things he could see outside the window.

The man in the other bed began to live for those one-hour periods where his world would be broadened and enlivened by all the activity and color of the world outside.

The window overlooked a park with a lovely lake, the man had said. Ducks and swans played on the water while children sailed their model boats. Young lovers walked arm in arm amidst flowers of every color and a fine view of the city skyline could be seen in the distance.

As the man by the window described all this in exquisite(精致的)detail, the man on the other side of the room would close his eyes and imagine the picturesque scene.

10

One warm afternoon the man by the window described a parade passing by. Although the other man couldn't hear the band, he could see it. In his mind's eye as the gentleman by the window portrayed it with descriptive words.

Days and weeks passed. One morning, the day nurse arrived to bring water for their baths only to find the lifeless body of the man by the window, who had died peacefully in his sleep. She was saddened and called the hospital attendants(服务员) to take the body away.

As soon as it seemed appropriate(适当的), the other man asked if he could be moved next to the window. The nurse was happy to make the switch, and after making sure he was comfortable, she left him alone.

Slowly, painfully, he propped(支撑) himself up on one elbow to take his first look at the real world outside. He strained(使劲) to slowly turn to look out the window beside the bed. It faced a blank(空白的) wall.

The man asked the nurse what could have compelled(强迫) his deceased(死者) roommate who had described such wonderful things outside this window. The nurse responded that the man was blind and could not even see the wall. She said, "Perhaps he just wanted to encourage you."
(477 words)

(Extracted from "http://sl.iciba.com/viewthread-19-202846-1.shtml")

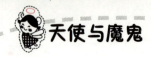

窗口

两个重病号住在同一间病房。一个每天下午能够在床上坐起来一个小时，以便排出肺部的流质物体。他的床靠着这间房子的惟一一扇窗户。另一个人只能平躺在床上度日。

两个人每天聊好几个小时。他们谈论自己的妻子和家人，谈论家庭、工作，参军的经历，还有好多其他的事情。每天下午，靠着窗户的那个人能坐起来的时候，总是向他的室友描绘他看到的窗外发生的所有事情。

睡在另一张床上的人开始盼望那些一小时的生活。每当那时窗外的一切活动和多姿多彩都让他感到视野开阔、心情愉快。

窗边的人说，从窗口望去是一个公园，里面有个可爱的池塘。鸭子和天鹅在水中嬉戏，孩子们则在操纵船模，年轻的恋人手挽手在绚丽多彩的花丛中散步，远处是城市地平线上美丽的风景。

靠窗的人用优美的语言详细描绘这些的时候，房子另一端的那个人就会闭上眼睛想象那些栩栩如生的情景。

一个温和的下午，窗口的那个人描绘了经过此处的游行。尽管另一个人没听到乐队演奏，但他却能看到。窗口那个人用生动的语言描绘的时候，他用心在看。

一天天过去了，一周周过去了。一天早晨，值白班的护士为他们提来洗澡水，看到的却是靠近窗口那个人的尸体，他在睡梦中安然去世了。她很悲伤，叫医院的值班人员把尸体抬走了。

一到合适的时机，另一个人便问他能否搬到窗口那儿去。护士很乐意为他做了调换，在确信他觉得舒适后，就离开了。

这个人用一个胳膊肘支撑着自己起来，想第一次亲眼看看外面的真实

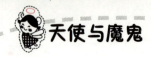

世界。他竭尽全力慢慢地朝床边的窗口望去，看到的却只是一面墙。

他问护士是什么促使他过世的室友描绘出窗外那么丰富的世界的。护士回答说，那个人是个盲人，甚至连墙都看不见。她说："也许他只是想鼓励你。"

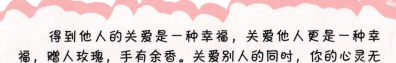

得到他人的关爱是一种幸福，关爱他人更是一种幸福，赠人玫瑰，手有余香。关爱别人的同时，你的心灵无疑也受到了爱的滋养，你的灵魂无疑也变得高贵。

关爱他人其实就是在关爱我们自己，关爱他人是我们得到他人关爱的前提。关爱是一片蔚蓝的天空，给予人们无限的希望；关爱是一盏明亮的灯，照亮人们美好的未来。

病友用自己的想象换回了同伴对生活的希望和对生命的希冀，他是天使，来到人间拨洒爱的种子。

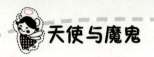

The Three Races
[之四]

> "Little boy, for this race you have won much more than in any race you have ever ran before, and for this race the crowd cheer not for any winner!"
>
> "孩子，这次比赛你比任何比赛赢得的都多。这次比赛人们不是为任何冠军而欢呼的！"

In old times, fable (寓言) tells the story of the young athletic boy hungry for success, for whom winning was everything and success was measured by such a result.

One day, a boy was preparing himself for a running competition in his small native village, himself and two other young boys to compete. A large crowd had congregated (聚集) to witness the sporting spectacle (壮观景象) and a wise old man, upon hearing of the little boy, had traveled far to bear witness also.

The race commenced (开始), but sure enough the boy called on his determination, strength and power. He took the winning line and was first. The crowd was ecstatic (狂喜的) and cheered and waved at the boy. The wise man remained still and calm, expressing no sentiment (观点). The little boy, however, felt proud and important.

A second race was called, and two new young, fit, challengers came forward, to run with the little boy. The race was started and sure enough the little boy came through and finished first once again. The crowd was ecstatic again and cheered and waved at the boy. The wise man remained still and calm, again expressing no sentiment. The little boy, however, felt proud and important.

天使与魔鬼

奉献天使篇

"Another race, another race!" pleaded the little boy. The wise old man stepped forward and presented the little boy with two new challengers, an elderly frail lady and a blind man. "What is this?" quizzed the little boy. "This is no race," he exclaimed. "Race!" said the wise man. The race was started and the boy was the only finisher, the other two challengers left standing at the starting line. The little boy was ecstatic; he raised his arms in delight. The crowd, however, was silent showing no sentiment toward the little boy.

"What has happened? Why not do the people join in my success?" he asked the wise old man. "Race again," replied the wise man, "This time, finish together, all three of you, finish together." The little boy thought a little, stood in the middle of the blind man and the frail old lady, and then took the two challengers by the hand. The race began and the little boy walked slowly, to the finishing line and crossed it. The crowd was ecstatic and cheered and waved at the boy. The wise man smiled, gently nodding his head. The little boy felt proud and important.

"Old man, I don't understand! Who is the crowd cheering for? Which one of us three?" asked the little boy. The wise old man looked into the little boy's eyes, placed his hands on the boy's shoulders, and replied softly. "Little boy, for this race you have won much more than in any race you have ever ran before, and for this race the crowd cheer not for any winner!" (495 words)

(Extracted from "http://www.rogerdarlington.me.uk/stories.html#Story50")

15

三次比赛

过去，寓言总是告诉人们年轻的运动员渴望成功，获得胜利就是一切，成功也是由胜利的结果来衡量的。

有一天，一个男孩和其他两个男孩在自己家乡的小村庄里准备赛跑，一大群观众聚集在一旁见证这一运动赛事。一位年长的智者听说这个小孩的事后，也大老远专程前来观看。

比赛开始了，男孩下定决心、集中力气和能量，冲向终点赢得第一。观众狂喜向男孩欢呼招手，智者依然平和冷静，没有表达任何观点，小男孩却很骄傲，觉得自己很重要。

第二次比赛准备开始，两名又年轻、又健壮的新挑战者走上前来，和小男孩一起比赛。比赛开始了，当然小男孩又一次冲了过去再次获得冠军。人群狂喜向男孩欢呼招手，智者仍然平和冷静，没有表达任何观点，而小男孩还很骄傲，觉得自己很重要。

"再来一次、再来一次！"小男孩请求道。智者向前走了一步，给小男孩领来两名新的挑战者，一位年长体弱的老妇和一位盲人。"这是什么？"小男孩问道。"这不是比赛，"他喊道。智者说："比赛！"比赛开始了，男孩是惟一一个抵达终点的选手，其他两名挑战者仍站在起点。小男孩大喜过望，高兴地举起双臂。但是这次人群却安静了，没有对男孩表示任何评论。

"怎么了？为什么大家不来庆祝我的成功？"他问智者。"再比一次。"智者回答，"这一次，一起到达终点，你们三个一起。"男孩想了一会儿，站在盲人和体弱老妇中间，然后手挽着两名挑战者。比赛开始了，小男孩慢慢地走着，穿过了终点。人群狂喜，向男孩欢呼招手。智者微笑着，轻轻点了点头。小男孩再次感到骄傲和重要。

"老人，我不明白。人们在欢呼什么？我们三个谁赢了？"男孩子问。老年智者看着孩子的眼睛，把双手放在孩子肩头，轻声回答："孩子，这次比赛你比任何比赛赢得的都多。这次比赛人们不是为任何冠军而欢呼的！"

如果你对人友善，处处为别人着想，并总是显得很开心，你就会发现别人会回报你的善意，你的快乐也会在别人身上体现出来。

奉献者收获的是一种幸福，一种崇高的情感，是他人的尊敬与爱戴，是自己生命的延续。人所能得到的最大的幸福、最自由快乐的心境，莫过于无私地奉献。修炼无私奉献的精神吧，它是幸福的源泉！

帮助那些需要帮助的人，让生活充满七彩的阳光！奉献天使是上天派来的使者，它捧出爱心，温暖人间。有天使经过的地方总有欢乐和微笑。

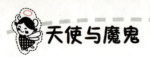

 奉献天使篇

[之五]

Another Kind of Joy

All this happened a long time ago, but the memory of it remains clear. That was the Christmas when my sisters and I learned the joy of making others happy.

这些都是很久很久以前的事了，然而回忆起来还是那么清晰。因为在那个圣诞日我和我的姐妹体会到了让别人快乐而获得的喜悦。

A light drizzle (毛毛细雨) was falling as my sister Jill and I ran out of the church, we were eager to get home to play with the presents that Santa had left for us and our baby sister, Sharon. Across the street from the church was a Pan American gas station where the Greyhound bus stopped. It was closed for Christmas, but I noticed a family standing outside the locked door, huddled (挤成一堆) under the narrow overhang (檐篷) in an attempt to keep dry.

As we drove down the highway through town, I noticed that the family was still there, standing outside the closed gas station.

My father was driving very slowly down the highway. The closer we got to the turnoff (分岔路口) for my grandparents' house, the slower the car went. Suddenly, my father U-turned (180度转弯) in the middle of the road and said, "I can't stand it! It's those people back there at the Pan Am, standing in the rain. They've got children. It's Christmas. I can't stand it."

When my father pulled into the service station, I saw that there were five of them: the parents and three children – two girls and a small boy.

My father rolled down his window. "Merry Christmas," he said.

"Howdy," the man replied.

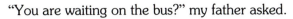

"You are waiting on the bus?" my father asked.

The man said that they were. They were going to Birmingham, where he had a brother. "Well, that bus isn't going to come along for several hours, and you're getting wet standing here. Winborn's just a couple miles up the road. They've got a shed (棚屋) with a cover there, and some benches," my father said. "Why don't you all get in the car and I'll run you up there."

The man thought about it for a moment, and then he beckoned (召唤) to his family. They climbed into the car. Once they settled in, my father looked back over his shoulder and asked the children if Santa had found them yet. Three glum (闷闷不乐的) faces mutely (缄默地) gave him his answer.

"Well, I don't think so," my father said, winking at my mother, "Because when I saw Santa this morning, he told me that he was having trouble finding all, and he asked me if he could leave your toys at my house. We'll just go to get them before I take you to the bus stop."

All at once, the three children's faces lit up, and they began to bounce around in the back seat, laughing and chattering.

When we got out of the car at our house, the three children ran through the front door and straight to the toys that were spread out under our Christmas tree. One of the girls spied Jill's doll and immediately hugged it to her breast. I remember that the little boy grabbed (突然抓住) Sharon's ball. And the other girl picked up something of mine. All this happened a long time ago, but the memory of it remains clear. That was the Christmas when my sisters and I learned the joy of making others happy. (554 words)

(Extracted from "http://www.hxen.com/englisharticle/prose/2009-05-18/77144_2.html")

另一种快乐

天上下着毛毛细雨，我和姐姐吉尔跑出教堂，只盼着快点回到家玩圣诞老人给我们和小妹妹莎伦准备的礼物玩具。教堂的对面是泛美油站，灰狗长途汽车会在那里中途停站。因为是圣诞节，那天油站没开，不过我发现在紧锁的站门外站着一家人，他们挤在狭小的

檐篷下，想尽量不被雨淋湿。

在开车经过刚才那条大路时，我看到那一家人仍然站在紧闭的油站门外。

在主干道上爸爸把车开得很慢。越接近去爷爷奶奶家的分岔路口，车子就越慢。突然，爸爸在半路中途来了个180度转弯，把车子原路驶回，他说："我实在不忍心！那几个在雨中站在泛美油站外的人。他们还带着小孩呢。圣诞节当前，我真的不忍心啊。"

爸爸把车开到油站旁停下，我看见那一家总共有5个人：父母俩和三个孩子--两个女孩跟一个小男孩。

爸爸摇下车窗对他们说："圣诞快乐！"

"你好，"那个男人回了一句。

"你们在等汽车吗？"爸爸问他们。

男人回答说是，他们准备去伯明翰，他有个哥哥在那边。爸爸说"汽车起码要好几个小时后才到这里，站在这儿等车你们都会淋湿的。往前几英里就是温邦站，那儿有个棚屋，有地方避雨，还有些长凳。不如上车我送你们到那里吧。"

男人想了一下之后示意他家人过来。等他们上车坐好了，爸爸转过头来

问那几个孩子，圣诞老人找到他们没有。三张忧郁的脸无声地回答了他。

"好吧，我不这样认为，"爸爸冲着妈妈眨着眼睛说："因为今早我见到圣诞老人时，他告诉我他没法找到所有人，还问我是否可以把你们的玩具礼物放在我家。在去公交车站之前我们先回去拿礼物吧。"

三个孩子的脸顿时阴霾尽散，还在后排座位蹦蹦跳跳，大笑大嚷起来。

到了我家一下车，那三个孩子穿过大门，直奔摆在圣诞树下的礼物。其中一个小女孩发现了吉尔的洋娃娃礼物，马上把它抱入怀中。我记得那小男孩抓走了莎伦的小球，而另外一个女孩就挑走了一件我的东西。这些都是很久很久以前的事了，然而回忆起来还是那么清晰。因为在那个圣诞日我和我的姐妹体会到了让别人快乐而获得的喜悦。

通往快乐的道路有很多条，我们偶尔也要改变一下方向，选择另一条通往快乐的路。文中并不富裕的一家人，慷慨地把自己的圣诞礼物送给了更需要的人。然而，他们并没有因此而感到失落，而是为了能够帮到别人而感到更加幸福。

如果世界是一间小屋，那关爱就是小屋中的一扇窗；如果世界是一艘船，那关爱就是茫茫大海上的一盏明灯。被人关爱是一种美好的享受，关爱他人是一种高尚的品德。

关爱，就是关心和爱护，它渗透在我们生活中的点点滴滴。生活中的每个人都需要关爱，正如植物的生长离不开阳光一样。我们只有不计回报地关心爱护他人，世界才会聚起爱的洪流，充满爱的天使！

21

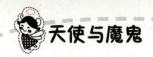

勇气天使篇
[之一]

The Power of Courage:
Glenn Cunningham's Story

> Still later in Madison Square Garden this young man who was not expected to survive, who would surely never walk, who could never hope to run – this determined young man, Dr. Glenn Cunningham, ran the world's fastest mile!
>
> 后来，在麦迪逊广场花园，这个没想到会活下来、肯定无法行走、更别梦想跑步的意志坚定的年轻人——格兰·坎宁安博士，打破了一英里的世界纪录！

The little country schoolhouse (校舍) was heated by an old–fashioned, pot–bellied (大肚子) coal stove. A little boy had the job of coming to school early each day to start the fire and warm the room before his teacher and his classmates arrived.

One morning the teachers and students arrived to find the schoolhouse engulfed (吞没) in flames. They dragged the unconscious little boy out of the flaming building more dead than alive. He had major burns over the lower half of his body and was taken to a nearby county hospital.

From his bed the dreadfully burned, semi–conscious little boy faintly heard the doctor talking to his mother. The doctor told his mother that her son would surely die – which was for the best, really – for the terrible fire had devastated (彻底摧毁) the lower half of his body.

But the brave boy didn't want to die. He made up his mind that he would survive. Somehow, to the amazement of the physician, he did survive. When the mortal danger was past, he again heard the doctor and his mother speaking quietly. The mother was told that since the fire had destroyed so much flesh in the lower part of his body, it would almost be better if he had died, since he was doomed to be a lifetime cripple with no use at all of his lower limbs.

Once more the brave boy made up his mind. He would not be a cripple. He would walk. But unfortunately from the waist down, he had no motor ability. His thin legs just dangled there, all but lifeless.

Ultimately he was released from the hospital. Every day his mother would massage his little legs, but there was no feeling, no control, nothing. Yet his determination that he would walk was as strong as ever.

When he wasn't in bed, he was confined（限制于）to a wheelchair. One sunny day his mother wheeled him out into the yard to get some fresh air. This day, instead of sitting there, he threw himself from the chair. He pulled himself across the grass, dragging his legs behind him.

He worked his way to the white fence bordering. With great effort, he raised himself up on the fence. Then, stake（栏杆）by stake, he began dragging himself along the fence, resolved that he would walk. He started to do this every day until he wore a smooth path all around the yard beside the fence. There was nothing he wanted more than to develop life in those legs.

Ultimately through his daily massages, his iron persistence and his resolute determination, he did develop the ability to stand up, then to walk haltingly, then to walk by himself – and then – to run.

He began to walk to school, then to run to school, to run for the sheer joy of running. Later in college he made the track team.

Still later in Madison Square Garden this young man who was not expected to survive, who would surely never walk, who could never hope to run – this determined young man, Dr. Glenn Cunningham, ran the world's fastest mile! (544 words)

(Extracted from "http://www.gagirl.com/stories/the-power-of-determination.html")

23

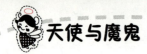

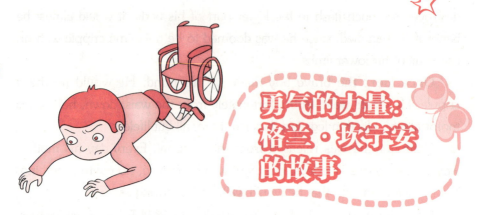

勇气的力量：格兰·坎宁安的故事

有一所乡村校舍用老式的大肚煤炉生火取暖。一个小男孩每天早晨提前到学校生火，在老师和同学们到来之前让房间里变得暖和一些。

一天早晨，师生们到学校时发现校舍被熊熊烈火吞没。他们把失去知觉的小男孩从火中救出来时，他已经奄奄一息。他的下半身严重烧伤，人们把他送往附近的一个乡村医院。

被严重烧伤、神志不清的小男孩躺在床上，模糊地听到医生在对他母亲说话。医生告诉他母亲，他儿子难逃一死——这已经是老天慈悲了——因为可怕的大火已经烧坏了他的下半身。

但勇敢的小男孩并不想死，他决心活下来。不知何故，让医生惊讶不已的是，他居然活了下来。当危险期过去之后，他又听到医生对他母亲悄悄说：因为大火吞噬了他下肢的许多肌肉，他要是真死了倒好了，这下他注定一辈子残疾，无法再活动他的双腿。

勇敢的男孩再一次下定决心。他不想做一辈子残疾，他要走路。但不幸的是，他腰部以下无法活动。他细瘦的双腿在那里摇摇晃晃，却一点儿也没有知觉。

他终于出院了。每天他母亲都为他按摩双腿，但他毫无知觉，也无法控制双腿。然而他再次站起来的决心依然那么坚定。

除了在床上的时候，他就坐在一张轮椅中。一天，阳光明媚，他母亲推着轮椅，让他到院子里呼吸新鲜空气。这一天，他不再坐在轮椅里，而是用自己的上身扑下轮椅，拖着双腿，在草地上爬行。

他爬到院子的白色围栏边，费力地抓住围栏，让自己的身体直立起来。然后，一根栏杆接着一根栏杆，他开始拉住围栏把自己向前拖，一边心中想着自己一定会走。他每天开始这样锻炼，直到院子的围栏边拖出了一条小径。他最渴望的就是开始站起来行走的人生。

最后，通过每日按摩和钢铁般的毅力和决心，他终于能够自己站立了，接着，他可以自己摇摇晃晃地行走--接着--他可以自己奔跑了。

他开始步行去学校，然后跑步上学，他跑步只是为了那种飞跑的快乐。在大学里，他入选校田径队。

后来，在麦迪逊广场花园，这个没想到会活下来、肯定无法行走、更别梦想跑步的意志坚定的年轻人——格兰·坎宁安博士，打破了一英里的世界纪录！

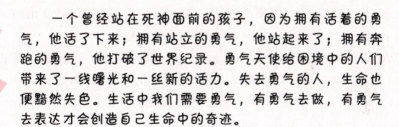

一个曾经站在死神面前的孩子，因为拥有活着的勇气，他活了下来；拥有站立的勇气，他站起来了；拥有奔跑的勇气，他打破了世界纪录。勇气天使给困境中的人们带来了一线曙光和一丝新的活力。失去勇气的人，生命也便黯然失色。生活中我们需要勇气，有勇气去做，有勇气去表达才会创造自己生命中的奇迹。

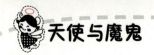

 勇气天使篇
[之二]

Run Through the Rain

> To everything there is a season and a time to every purpose under heaven. I hope you still take the time to run through the rain.
>
> 世间万物皆有自己的季节，做任何事情也有一个恰当的时机。希望你有机会在雨中狂奔一回。

She had been shopping with her Mom in Wal-Mart. She must have been 6 years old, this beautiful brown haired, freckle-faced image of innocence（天真）. It was pouring outside. The kind of rain that gushes over the top of rain gutters（屋顶的檐槽）, so much in a hurry to hit the Earth, it has no time to flow down the spout（喷出的水柱）.

We all stood there under the awning（遮篷）and just inside the door of the Wal-Mart. We all waited, some patiently, others irritated, because nature messed up（弄乱, 弄糟）their hurried day. I am always mesmerized by rainfall. I get lost in the sound and sight of the heavens washing away the dirt and dust of the world. Memories of running, splashing so carefree as a child come pouring in as a welcome reprieve from the worries of my day.

Her voice was so sweet as it broke the hypnotic trance we were all caught in, "Mom, let's run through the rain," she said.

"What?" Mom asked.

"Let's run through the rain!" she repeated.

"No, honey. We'll wait until it slows down a bit," Mom replied.

This young child waited about another minute and repeated, "Mom, let's run through the rain."

"We'll get soaked if we do," Mom said.

"No, we won't, Mom. That's not what you said this morning," the young girl said as she tugged at her Mom's arm.

"This morning? When did I say we could run through the rain and not get wet?"

"Don't you remember? When you were talking to Daddy about his cancer, you said, 'If God can get us through this, he can get us through anything!'"

The entire crowd stopped dead silent. I swear you couldn't hear anything but the rain. We all stood silently. No one came or left in the next few minutes. Mom paused and thought for a moment about what she would say.

Now some would laugh it off and scold her for being silly. Some might even ignore what was said. But this was a moment of affirmation in a young child's life. Time when innocent trust can be nurtured so that it will bloom into faith. "Honey, you are absolutely right. Let's run through the rain. If get wet, well maybe we just needed washing," Mom said. Then off they ran.

We all stood watching, smiling and laughing as they darted past the cars. They held their shopping bags over their heads just in case. They got soaked. But they were followed by a few who screamed and laughed like children all the way to their cars. And yes, I did. I ran. I got wet. I needed washing. Circumstances (环境) or people can take away your material possessions, they can take away your money, and they can take away your health. But no one can ever take away your precious memories. So, don't forget to make time and take the opportunities to make memories every day!

To everything there is a season and a time to every purpose under heaven. I hope you still take the time to run through the rain. (511 words)

(Extracted from "http://www.51test.net/show/456098.html")

27

雨中狂奔

她和妈妈刚在沃尔玛结束购物。这个天真的小女孩应该6岁大了，一头美丽的棕发，脸上有雀斑。外面下着倾盆大雨。雨水溢满了屋顶的檐槽，来不及排走，就迫不及待地涌涨上地面。

我们都站在沃尔玛门口的遮篷下。大家都在等待，有人很耐心，有人很烦躁，因为老天在给他们本已忙碌的一天添乱。雨天总引起我的遐思。我出神地听着、看着老天冲刷洗涤这世界的污垢和尘埃，儿时无忧无虑地在雨中奔跑玩水的记忆汹涌而至，暂时缓解了我一天的焦虑。

小女孩甜美的声音打破了这令人昏昏欲睡的气氛，"妈妈，我们在雨里跑吧。"她说。

"什么？"母亲问。

"我们在雨里跑吧！"她重复了一遍。

"不，宝贝。我们等雨小一点再走，"母亲回答说。

过了一会儿小女孩又说："妈妈，我们跑出去吧。"

"这样的话我们会湿透的，"母亲说。

"不会的，妈妈。你今天早上不是这样说的，"小女孩一边说一边拉着母亲的手。

"今天早上？我什么时候说过我们淋雨不会湿啊？"

"你不记得了吗？你和爸爸说起他的癌症时，你不是说'如果上帝让我们闯过这一关，那我们就没有什么过不去的了。'"

人群一片寂静。我发誓，除了雨声，你什么都听不到。我们都静静地站着。接下来的几分钟没有一个人走动。母亲停了一下，想着应该说些什么。

有人也许会对此一笑了之，或是责备这孩子不懂事，有人甚至把她的话当作耳旁风。但这却是一个孩子一生中需要得到肯定的时候。如果受到鼓舞，这时孩子单纯的信任就会发展成为坚定的信念。"宝贝，你说得对，我们跑过去吧。如果淋湿了，那也许是因为我们的确需要冲洗一下了，"母亲说。然后她们就冲出去了。

我们站在那儿，笑着看她们飞奔过停着的汽车。她们举起购物袋想挡挡雨，但还是湿透了。好几个人像孩子般尖叫着，大笑着，也跟着冲了出去，奔向自己的车子。当然，我也跑了出去，淋湿了。我也需要接受洗礼。环境或者别人可以夺去你的物质财富，抢走你的金钱，带走你的健康，但没有人能带走你珍贵的回忆。因此，记得要抓紧时间，抓住机会，每天都给自己留下一些回忆吧！

世间万物皆有自己的季节，做任何事情也有一个恰当的时机。希望你有机会在雨中狂奔一回。

人类所有的力量，都是耐心加上时间的混合，所谓勇者，是既有意志，又能等待时机的人。勇气的底蕴是智慧，没有智慧做支撑的勇者，充其量只能算作是莽夫一个，炮灰而已。勇气天使在时刻提醒着我们：记得要有勇气抓紧时间，抓住机会，每天都给自己留下一些回忆吧！留住勇气的金钥匙是信念，只有心中怀有坚定的信念，勇气才会呼之欲出。

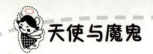

勇气天使篇
[之三]

Mom's Answer

When the waves come near, little birds can rise quickly while "clumsy" sea-gulls would take more time to complete the process. However, have you noticed birds that finally fly across the endless ocean are none other than "clumsy" sea-gulls?

当海浪打来的时候，小麻雀总能迅速地起飞，而海鸥总显得非常笨拙，它们从沙滩飞入天空总要很长时间。然而，真正能飞越广阔大海的还是那些"笨拙"的海鸥。

For long, a little boy was wondering why his next-desk-pal（同桌）could rank 1st in the class whenever he wanted to, whereas he himself failed to: he only ranked 21st.

At home, he asked his Mom, "Mom, am I more stupid than others? I feel I am as obedient and as careful as him, but how come I always lag behind?" Hearing the words, Mom was aware that her son began to gain amour-propre（自尊心）, which was now being undermined by the ranking system. Staring at him, she went wordless, not knowing how to explain.

In another test, the son ranked 17th, while his pal remained 1st. Back home, he raised the same question. Mom really wanted to inform her son that intelligence differs, which means that students ranking 1st are supposed to be cleverer than normal ones. However, was this disillusioning（幻灭的）answer the one that her son was constantly curious about? Thank goodness she did not open her mouth.

How to answer her son's question? There were times she felt an impulse to equivocate（使用模棱两可的话隐瞒真相）, "You are too lazy. You are not as industrious as others…" But she stopped while envisioning her son suffering from the pains of unsatisfied grades and rankings. She thought it cruel to inflict any additional burdens on her son and was trying to find out a perfect answer.

Time elapsing swiftly, the son finished primary school. Despite studying harder and better, he was still unable to keep up with his pal. To show her pride of him, Mom decided to take him to the sea. During the trip, she managed to give out an answer.

Now, the son no longer worries about his rankings, and there are no longer boring guys who would inquire his rankings in primary school, because, with the 1st ranking, he is accepted by Tsinghua University.

Back home in winter vacation, he was invited to address the students and parents in his high school. In the speech, he mentioned a valuable experience in his childhood, "…When my mother and I was sitting on the beach, she pointed to the front and said, 'Do you see the seabirds scrambling （争夺, 争抢）for food over there? When the waves come near, little birds can rise quickly while 'clumsy'（笨拙的）sea-gulls would take more time to complete the process. However, have you noticed birds that finally fly across the endless ocean are none other than 'clumsy' sea-gulls?'"

The moving speech provoked many mothers present into tears, including his. (409 words)

31

妈妈的答案

有个孩子对一个问题一直想不通：为什么他的同桌想考第一就考了第一名，而自己想考第一却只考了全班第二十一名？

回家后，他问道："妈妈我是不是比别人笨？我觉得我和他一样听话，一样认真，可是，为什么我总是落在他后面？"妈妈听了儿子的话，意识到儿子开始有自尊心了，而这种自尊心正在被学校的排名伤害着。她望着儿子，没有回答，因为她也不知道怎样回答。

又一次考试后，孩子考了第十七名，而他的同桌还是第一名。回家后，儿子又问了同样的问题。她真想说，人的智力确实不同，考第一的人，脑子就是比一般的人聪明。然而这样打击人的回答，难道是孩子真想知道的答案吗？她庆幸自己没说出口。

应该怎样回答儿子的问题呢？有几次，她真想搪塞儿子说："你太贪玩了；你还不够努力……"想到儿子为成绩和排名而痛苦的样子，她没有说话。给儿子再增加额外的负担太残酷了。她想为儿子的问题找到一个完美的答案。

时光飞逝，儿子小学毕业了，虽然他比过去更加刻苦，学习也进步了。但依然没有赶上他的同桌。为了对儿子的进步表示赞赏，她决定带他去看一次大海。就是在这次旅行中，这位母亲回答了儿子的问题。

现在，这位做儿子的再也不担心自己的名次了，也再没有人无聊地追问他小学时成绩排第几名，因为他去年以全校第一名的成绩考入了清华。

寒假归来时，母校请他给同学及家长们做一个报告。其中他讲了小时候的一段珍贵的经历："……我和母亲坐在沙滩上，她指着前面对我说，'你看那些在海边争食的鸟儿，当海浪打来的时候，小灰雀总能迅速地起飞，而海鸥总显得非常笨拙，它们从沙滩飞入天空总要很长时间。然而，真正能飞越广阔大海的还是那些'笨拙'的海鸥。'"

这个报告让很多母亲流下了眼泪，其中也包括他自己的母亲。

母亲对孩子意味深长地说："当海浪打来的时候，小灰雀总能迅速地起飞，它们拍打两三下翅膀就升入天空；而海鸥总显得非常笨拙，它们从沙滩飞入天空总要很长时间；然而，真正能飞越大海横过大洋的还是它们。"如果不敢去跑，就不可能赢得竞赛；如果不敢去战斗，就不可能赢得胜利；如果不去勇敢地尝试飞翔，就不可能拥有整片天空。记住，勇气天使永远都会在我们的身边，只要你需要它，就去召唤它吧！

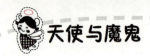

勇气天使篇
[之四]

The Firm Helen Keller

Luckily, Helen was not someone who gave up easily.

万幸的是，海伦并不是个轻易认输的人。

In 1882, a baby girl caught a fever which was so fierce that she nearly died. She survived but the fever left its mark–she could no longer see or hear. Because she could not hear she also found it very difficult to speak.

So how did this child, blinded and deafened at 19 months old, grow up to become a world–famous author and public speaker?

The fever cut her off from the outside world, depriving her of sight and sound. It was as if she had been thrown into a dark prison cell from which there could be no release.

Luckily, Helen was not someone who gave up easily. Soon she began to explore the world by using her other senses. She followed her mother wherever she went, hanging onto her skirts. She touched and smelled everything she came across. She copied their actions and was soon able to do certain jobs herself, like milking the cows or kneading dough（揉面）. She even learnt to recognize people by feeling their faces or their clothes. She could also tell where she was in the garden by the smell of the different plants and the feel of the ground under her feet.

By the age of seven she had invented over 60 different signs by which she could talk to her families. If she wanted bread for example, she would pretend to cut a loaf and butter the slices. If she wanted ice cream she wrapped her arms around herself and pretended to shiver.

Helen was unusual in that she was extremely intelligent and also remarkably sensitive. By her own efforts she had managed to make some sense of an alien and confusing world. But even so she had limitations.

At the age of five Helen began to realize she was different from other people. She noticed that her family did not use signs like she did but talked with their mouths. Sometimes she stood between two people and touched their lips. She could not understand what they said and she could not make any meaningful sounds herself. She wanted to talk but no matter how she tried she could not make herself understood. This makes her so angry that she used to hurl herself around the room, kicking and screaming in frustration (失意；沮丧).

As she got older her frustration grew and her rages became worse and worse. She became wild and unruly. If she didn't get what she wanted she would throw tantrums (突然发怒) until her family gave in. Her favorite tricks included grabbing other people's food from their plates and hurling fragile (易碎的) objects to the floor. Once she even managed to lock her mother into the pantry (厨房). Eventually it became clear that something had to be done. So, just before her seventh birthday, the family hired a private tutor –Anne Sullivan.

Anne was careful to teach Helen especially those subjects in which she was interested. As a result Helen became gentler and she soon learnt to read and write in Braille（布莱叶盲文）. She also learnt to read people's lips by pressing her finger–tips against them and feeling the movement and vibrations（震动）. This method is called Tadoma and it is a skill that very, very few people manage to acquire. She also learnt to speak, a major achievement for someone who could not hear at all.

Helen proved to be a remarkable scholar, graduating with honours from Radcliffe College in 1904. She had phenomenal（惊人的）powers of concentration and memory, as well as a dogged determination to succeed. While she was still at college she wrote *The Story of My Life*. This was an immediate success and earned her enough money to buy her own house.

She toured the country, giving lecture after lecture. Many books were

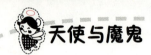
written about her and several plays and films were made about her life. Eventually she became so famous that she was invited abroad and received many honours from foreign universities and monarchs（君主，帝王）. In 1932, she became a vice-president of the Royal National Institute for the Blind in the United Kingdom.

After her death in 1968 an organization was set up in her name to combat blindness in the developing world. Today that agency, Helen Keller International, is one of the biggest organizations working with blind people overseas. (708 words)

(Extracted from "http://www.englishchina.com/celeb/23.htm")

坚强的 海伦·凯勒

1882年，一名女婴因发烧险些丧命。她虽然幸存下来，但是发烧给她留下了后遗症——她从此失明变聋。因为耳聋，她连讲话也变得很困难。

那么这样一个在19个月时就既盲又聋的孩子，是如何成长为享誉世界的作家和演说家的呢？

高烧夺去了她的视力和声音，将她与外界隔开。她仿佛置身在黑暗的牢笼中无法摆脱。

万幸的是，海伦并不是个轻易认输的人。不久她就开始利用其他的感官来探索这个世界了。她跟着母亲，拉着母亲的裙角，形影不离。她用触觉和嗅觉去感知各种她碰到的物品。她模仿别人的动作并且很快就能自己做一些事情，例如挤牛奶或揉面。她甚至学会通过摸别人的脸或衣服来识别对方。她还能闻出不同的植物和触摸地面来辨别自己在花园的位置。

七岁的时候她发明了60多种不同的手势和家人交流。例如她要是想吃面包，就会做出切面包和涂黄油的动作。想吃冰淇淋时就用胳膊抱住自己装出发抖的样子。

海伦在这方面非比一般，她绝顶聪明又相当敏感。通过努力她对这个陌生且迷惑的世界有了一些认知。但她仍有一些局限。

五岁时海伦开始意识到她与别人不同。她发现家里的其他人不用像她那样做手势而是用嘴交谈。有时她站在两人中间触摸他们的嘴唇。不知道他们在说什么，而她自己不能发出有意义的声音。她想讲话，可无论费多大的劲儿也无法使别人明白自己。这让她异常懊恼，常常在屋子里乱跑乱撞，沮丧地又踢又喊。

随着年龄的增长她越来越灰心，越来越愤怒，她变得狂野不驯。倘若她得不到想要的东西就会大发脾气直到家人顺从为止。她最喜欢抓别人盘里的食物，将易碎的东西猛扔在地。有一次她甚至将母亲锁在厨房里。这样一来就得想个办法了。于是，在她快到七岁生日时，家里便雇了一名家庭教师——安尼·沙利文。

安尼细心地教授海伦，特别是她感兴趣的东西。海伦变得温和了，很快还学会了用布莱叶盲文朗读和写作。也学会了用手指接触说话人的嘴唇去感受运动和震动，她学会了读唇语。这种方法叫"多码"，是一种极少有人掌握的技能。她也学会了讲话，这对失聪的人来说是个巨大的成就。

海伦证明了自己是个出色的学者，1904年她以优异的成绩从拉德克利夫学院毕业。她有惊人的注意力和记忆力，同时她还具有不达目的誓不罢休的毅力。上大学时她就写了《我的生命》，这使她取得了巨大的成功，用赚的钱为自己购买了一套住房。

她周游全国，不断地举行讲座。她的事迹被许多人著书立说，还被搬上了舞台和银幕。最终她声名显赫，应邀出国并受到外国大学和国王授予的荣誉。1932年，她成为英国皇家国立盲人学院的副校长。

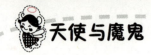

1968年她去世后，成立了一个以她的名字命名的组织，该组织旨在与发展中国家存在的失明缺陷做斗争。如今这所机构，"海伦·凯勒国际基金会"，是海外向盲人提供帮助的最大组织之一。

海伦·凯勒，一个独特的生命个体，一个生活在黑暗中却又给人类带来光明的女性，以其自强不息的毅力，以其勇敢的心灵震撼了世界。她接受了生命的挑战，用爱心去拥抱世界，以惊人的毅力面对困境，终于在黑暗中找到了人生的光明面，最后又把慈爱的双手伸向全世界。海伦不正是我们要寻找的这位美丽的勇气天使吗？

勇气天使篇

[之五]

Attacked by a Butterfly

Since then, I've always tried to remember the courage of that butterfly whenever I see huge obstacles facing me. I use that butterfly's courage as an inspiration and to remind myself that good things are worth fighting for.

此后，每当我遇到巨大的障碍，都会努力想起那只蝴蝶的勇气。我把他的勇气当成一种鼓舞，并提醒自己，好的东西是值得为之奋斗的。

Walking down a path through some woods in Georgia, I saw a water puddle(水坑) ahead on the path. I angled (表述) my direction to go around it on the part of the path that wasn't covered by water and mud. As I reached the puddle, I was suddenly attacked! Yet I did nothing for the attack was so unpredictable（不可预料的） and from a source so totally unexpected. I was startled as well as unhurt, in spite of having been struck four or five times already. I backed（后退） up a foot and my attacker stopped attacking me. Instead of attacking more, he hovered（徘徊） in the air on graceful butterfly wings in front of me. Had I been hurt I wouldn't have found it amusing, but I was unhurt, it was funny, and I was laughing. After all, I was being attacked by a butterfly!

Having stopped laughing, I took a step forward. My attacker rushed me again. He rammed（猛撞） me in the chest with his head and body, striking me over and over again with all his might, still to no avail. For a second time, I retreated a step while my attacker relented（变温和） in his

39

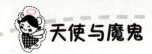
attack. Yet again, I tried moving forward. My attacker charged me again. I was rammed in the chest over and over again. I wasn't sure what to do, other than to retreat a third time. After all, it's just not everyday that one is attacked by a butterfly. This time, though, I stepped back several paces to look the situation over. My attacker moved back as well to land on the ground. That's when I discovered why my attacker was charging me only moments earlier. He had a mate and she was dying. She was beside the puddle where he landed.

Sitting close beside her, he opened and closed his wings as if to fan her. I could only admire the love and courage of that butterfly in his concern for his mate. He had taken it upon himself to attack me for his mate's sake, even though she was clearly dying and I was so large. He did so just to give her those extra few precious moments of life, should I have been careless enough to step on her. Now I knew why and what he was fighting for. There was really only one option left for me. I carefully made my way around the puddle to the other side of the path, though it was only inches wide and extremely muddy (泥泞的). His courage in attacking something thousands of times larger and heavier than himself just for his mate's safety justified (证明有道理) it. I couldn't do anything other than reward him by walking on the more difficult side of the puddle. He had truly earned those moments to be with her, undisturbed.

Since then, I've always tried to remember the courage of that butterfly whenever I see huge obstacles facing me. I use that butterfly's courage as an inspiration (妙计) and to remind myself that good things are worth fighting for. (551 words)

(Extracted from "http://www.crazyenglish.org/qingsongyingyu/wenku/20081102/35143.html")

遭遇蝴蝶袭击

　　我在佐治亚州沿着一条穿过几个树林的小径行走，发现前面路上有一个水坑。我转向路上没被水和泥覆盖的那部分，好绕过它。当我到达水坑的时候，我突然遭遇了袭击！但我置之不理，因为这种袭击如此不可预料，而且来自一个你完全想不到的袭击者。我很震惊，但没受伤，尽管我已经遭遇了四五次连续袭击。我后退了一步，袭击者也停止了进攻。它不再进攻，而是在我面前优美地扇动着翅膀翩然起舞。要是我受了伤，我就不会觉得这可笑了，可是我没有受伤，这很滑稽，我笑了起来。毕竟，我是被一只蝴蝶袭击了！

　　我止住笑声向前迈了一步。袭击者又冲向了我，用脑袋和身体撞击我的胸膛，一次又一次，竭尽全力却无济于事。我再一次后退了一步，与此同时，袭击者的攻击也减缓了。我再次尝试向前移动，袭击者也再次向我攻击。我的胸膛遭受了一次又一次的撞击，我不知道该怎么办，只好第三次向后退。毕竟人不是每天都会被蝴蝶袭击的。然而这次，我后退了好几步来审视情况。袭击者也退了回去，落在地面上。这时我发现了袭击者此前攻击我的原因。他的伴侣奄奄一息，就躺在他落下的泥坑旁边。

　　他紧靠在她的旁边，翅膀一张一合，好像在替她扇扇子。我只能钦佩那只蝴蝶在对他的伴侣的关心中表现出的爱和勇气。为了他的伴侣，他屡次对我发起袭击，即使她已明显接近死亡，而我又如此庞大。他这样做只是为了保住她生命中那额外一点珍贵时光，我真不该那么不小心差点踩到她。现在，我已知道他为何而战、为谁而战。我只有一个选择，我小心地绕到泥坑另一边的路上，尽管它只有几英寸宽而且相当泥泞。他为了伴侣的安全去攻击比自己大几千倍、重几千倍的对手，其中表现出的勇气证明

41

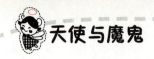

了他有正当的理由。我帮不上什么忙，除了走泥坑更难走的一边来奖励他。他真的赢得了和她在一起的、那不被打扰的片刻时光。

此后，每当我遇到巨大的障碍，都会努力想起那只蝴蝶的勇气。我把他的勇气当成一种鼓舞，并提醒自己，好的东西是值得为之奋斗的。

希望你能和作者一样，当遇到巨大的障碍时，会努力想起本文中这只蝴蝶的勇气。它是一只飞舞的勇气天使，请你把它的勇气当成一种鼓舞，并提醒自己，好的东西是值得为之奋斗的。

如果不敢去跑，就不可能赢得竞赛；如果你不敢去战斗，就不可能赢得胜利。歌德曾说："你若失掉了勇敢，你就会把一切失去。"

勇气是不限人的，任凭你是谁，只要你能够勇于面对自己，坦然面对天地，不惧，不恐，不惊，能够为了正义的事勇于献出一切，乃至于自己的性命，你便是有勇气的人，而你的精神，就是勇气！

宽容天使篇

[之一]

I'm Proud of You

> Yet it dwells in my memory that she taught me a lesson in forgiveness that I shall never forget.
>
> 不过，她曾给我上的那堂关于"宽恕"的课却始终让我难以忘怀。

Forty-three years seems like a long time to remember the name of a mere acquaintance (相识). I have forgotten the name of an old lady, who was a customer on the paper route in my home town when I was a twelve-year-old boy. Yet it dwells in my memory that she taught me a lesson in forgiveness that I shall never forget.

On a winter afternoon, a friend and I were throwing stones onto the slanted (倾斜的) roof of the old lady's house from a spot near her backyard. The object of our play was to observe how the stones changed to missiles as they rolled to the roof's edge and shot out into the yard like comets falling from the sky. I found myself a perfectly smooth rock and threw it out. The stone was too smooth, however, so it slipped from my hand as I let it go and headed straight not for the roof but for a small window on the old lady's back porch . At the sound of fractured (破碎的) glass, we knew we were in trouble. We turned tail and ran faster than any of our missiles flew off her roof.

I was too scared about getting caught that first night to be concerned about the old lady with the broken window in winter. However, a few days later, when I was sure that I hadn't been discovered, I started to feel guilty

43

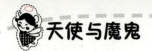
for her misfortune (不幸). She still greeted me with a smile each day when I gave her the paper, but I was no longer able to act comfortable in her presence.

I made up my mind that I would save my paper delivery money, and in three weeks I had the seven dollars that I calculated would cover the cost of her window. I put the money in an envelope with a note explaining that I was sorry for breaking her window and hoped that the seven dollars would cover the cost for repairing it.

I waited until it was dark, snuck up to the old lady's house, and put the letter I didn't sign through the letter slot in her door. My soul felt redeemed (赎罪了) and I could have the freedom of, once again, looking straight into the old lady's kind eyes.

The next day, I handed the old lady her paper and was able to return the warm smile that I was receiving from her. She thanked me for the paper and gave me a bag of cookies she had made herself. I thanked her and proceeded to eat the cookies as I continued my route.

After several cookies, I felt an envelope and pulled it out of the bag. When I opened the envelope, I was stunned (震惊的). Inside were the seven dollars and a short note that said, "I'm proud of you." (470 words)

(Extracted from "http://www.paedu.net/geyan/EnglishArticles/shuangyu/201006/45272.html")

为你骄傲

记住一个仅仅认识的人的名字，43年似乎是段很长的时间。我已经忘了那位老太太的名字，她是我12岁那年在家乡送报时的一位客户。不过，她曾给我上的那堂关于宽恕的课却始终让我难以忘怀。

一个冬天的下午，我和一个朋友在离这个老太太家屋后不远的一个地方往她家斜斜的屋顶上扔石子玩。我们的目的是观察这些石子如何顺着屋顶的斜坡变成一颗颗导弹，在滚落到屋顶边缘的瞬间，像滑过天空的彗星一样射入院中。我找到颗非常光滑的石子扔了出去。但是，这颗石子太光滑了，在出手的一刹那，它偏离了方向。没有落在屋顶上，反而直接击中了老太太屋后门廊上的一扇小窗户。听到玻璃破碎的声音，我们知道闯祸了。于是掉头拔腿就跑，跑得比任何一颗从她屋顶发射的石子都要快。

当天晚上，我太害怕被抓住，没有考虑到冬天里的破玻璃窗会给老太太带来什么样的麻烦。但是过了几天，我确信自己没被发现时，开始对给她带来的倒霉事感到内疚了。每天我给她送报纸时，她依旧笑眯眯地迎接我。不过，在她面前，我已经不像以前那样自在了。

我决定把送报挣的钱攒起来。三周后，我攒了7美元，我估算这大概够赔偿她的窗户了。便把钱装进一个信封，附上了一张纸条，解释说我对打破她家的窗户感到很抱歉，希望这7美元足够赔付修窗户的钱。

我一直等到天黑，才悄悄走到她家门前，把这封没有署名的信从信箱口投进了她家。做完这件事情后，我感到自己的灵魂好像得到了解脱，获得了新的自由，能够重新正视老太太慈祥的目光了。

第二天，当老人微笑着从我手上接过报纸时，我也能向她回报一个热

45

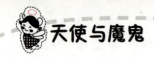

情的微笑。她对我的送报工作表示感谢，送了我一纸袋她亲手做的饼干。谢过她后，我一边吃着饼干，一边继续去给别的客户送报纸。

　　吃了几块饼干以后，我摸到了一个信封，就把它拽了出来。我打开信封时，我不禁怔住了。信封里有7美元和一张纸条，上面写道："我为你感到骄傲。"

　　如果爱是海洋，宽容就是一条奔流不息的河流，她让大海更加浩瀚。如果爱是春天，宽容就是呼唤春天而至的天使，她给春天带来绿意和芬芳。"我为你骄傲"，这朴素的语言中直接体现了容忍、谅解和鼓励。不同的读者，会用各异的方式来解读老妇人那颗宽容的心，然而我们共同的收获是在心中播下宽容的种子，这颗种子结出的果实一定是美好的、甘甜的。

宽容天使篇
[之二]

Forgiveness or Blame

> On the contrary, if you can drop your hate and fear, and look at it in another way, it may not be that bad as you imagined.
>
> 相反的，如果能放下怨恨和惧怕，换一个角度看事情，可能事情的境况并不如想象中那么糟。

One couple gave birth to a boy in the eleventh year of their marriage, and they loved him deeply.

When the boy was two years old, the husband saw an open bottle of liquid medicine on the table one morning, when he was about to leave for work. But he was in a hurry, so he told his wife loudly to put the medicine away and left.

The wife was so busy in the kitchen that she totally forgot about the medicine thing.

The little boy took up the bottle, attracted by the color of the liquid. He felt curious about it, so he drank up the medicine. Doses of the medicine ingredients(成份) were very high, even adults could only take a small amount.

The poor little boy overdosed (服药过量) himself, although taken to hospital in time, he still died.

The wife was frightened by what happened. She did not know how to face her husband, how hardly he would blame her!

The anxious father rushed to the hospital, just got the bad news. Standing beside their son's dead body, he looked at his wife, and told her: I

47

love you daring!

What simple words! But on that occasion, how much forgiveness and human wisdom were involved (包含) in them!

Facing an unfortunate event, you may be extremely angry, you can complain, even to blame others, but will things change a little? It will only hurt you in your rest life, like a scar (伤疤) on your body.

On the contrary, if you can drop your hate and fear, and look at it in another way, it may not be that bad as you imagined. (273 words)

(Extracted from "http://joanna-wang508.blog.sohu.com/171464227.html")

宽容还是责难

一对夫妇在婚后十一年生了一个男孩，夫妇二人深深地爱着他们的孩子。

男孩两岁的某一天早晨，丈夫出门上班时，看到桌上有一瓶打开盖子的药水。不过，因为赶时间，他只大声告诉妻子记得把药瓶收好，然后就关上门，上班去了。

妻子在厨房里忙得团团转，全然忘了丈夫的叮嘱。

小男孩拿起药瓶，被药水的颜色所吸引。他好奇地一口气喝光了药水。药水成份剂量很高，即使成人也只能服用少量。

男孩由于服药过量，虽然被及时送到医院，但仍旧回天乏术。

妻子被突如其来的意外吓呆了，不知如何面对丈夫，更不知道丈夫会如何责难她。

焦急的父亲赶到医院，得知噩耗非常伤心。他站在儿子的尸体旁，望了妻子一眼，然后说：亲爱的，我爱你！

多么简单的一句话！但要有多大的包容、多深的人生智慧，才能在那种时刻说出这样一句话。

面对一件不幸的事情，你可以大发雷霆，怨天尤人，甚至责难一干人等，但事情却不会因为这些而有丝毫改变。它只会在往后的生活继续伤害你，使你带着疤痕地活下去。

相反，如果能放下怨恨和惧怕，换一个角度看事情，可能事情的境况并不如想象中那么糟。

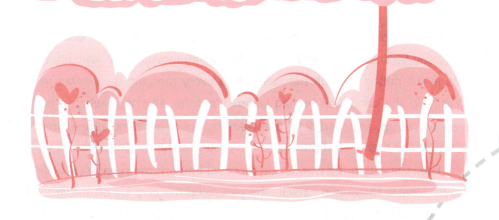

当我们选择宽容，天使已悄然而至。我们的心灵会把创伤抚平，我们的眼睛会将美景捕捉。宽容是人生智慧的体现，是人生阅历的沉淀，更是人生哲学的修炼。宽容，或大或小，都是雪中送炭。

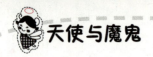

 宽容天使篇

[之三]

Why Forgive Yourself ?

> To forgive is to set a prisoner free and discover the prisoner was you.
>
> 原谅就是释放囚徒，然后发现那囚徒不是别人，正是自己。

Once upon a time there lived a woman who had a bad temper. She screamed at and scolded everyone around her. For most of her life she believed the fiery (暴躁的) rage inside her was everyone else's fault.

She went to see a well respected Buddhist monk to ask for advice. The monk told her to take a large clay jug from his kitchen, fill it with water, and stand outside on the sidewalk in front of his house. "It's hot outside, and that's a busy sidewalk with lots of pedestrians," the monk told her as he pointed out the front window of his house. "When a pedestrian passes, you must offer them a glass of water. Do this until there is no rage left inside you."

So she stood outside with a water jug and served water to pedestrians every day for the next several weeks. And every morning she asked herself if rage still pulsed through her veins. And every morning the answer was, "Yes." So she continued serving water. Until this afternoon when a burly man walked up, snatched(抢夺) the water jug out of her hand, drank directly out of it, and then tossed the jug on the ground as he continued on his way.

The rage within the woman skyrocketed into an irrepressible (抑制不住的) fit. Unable to contain herself, she picked up the clay jug off the ground and, with all her might, threw it at the burly man as he walked away. It was a direct hit. The jug shattered into pieces over the back of his head and he fell to the ground, unconscious and bleeding.

As the woman's rage subsided(平息), she realized the magnitude of what she had done and began to cry. She used a payphone to call 911 and report the incident. An ambulance and two police cars arrived at the scene moments later. As the EMTs strapped the burly man into a stretcher, the police handcuffed his arms and legs to the stretcher. Then one of the police officers walked over to the woman, who was still crying, and said, "The city owes you a big 'thank you'. That man has been on our most wanted list for over a year now. He is a primary suspect in multiple murder cases and violent robberies."

The moral of the story is that we simply don't know. We want to believe that if we completely rid ourselves of our inner darkness then we will always make the right choices, and be of service to ourselves and those around us. But life isn't so linear and predicable. Sometimes our darkness inadvertently (无意的) leads us to do things that impact the world in a positive way, just as our unconditional love sometimes forces us to overlook the criminal standing before us. (463 words)

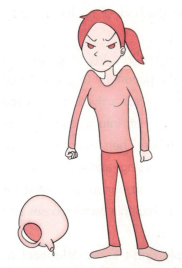

为什么你必须原谅自己

从前有个脾气很坏的女人，她总是对周围的人大喊大叫，认为她生气都是因为别人的错。

于是，她去请教一位德高望重的高僧。高僧让她从厨房取了一个很大的装满水的陶壶，提着站在外面的人行道上。"外面很热，行人很多，"高僧指着窗外说，"每一个行人经过你身边时，你都要给他们倒一杯水，直到你心中没有怒火为止。"

在接下来的几周里，她都拿着陶壶站在外面，给过往行人倒水。每天早晨，她都问自己：自己是否还有怒气，而每天她的回答都是肯定的。于是她继续这样为别人倒水。直到有一天下午，一个粗鲁的男人走过来，一把从她手里抢过陶壶，一口气喝完了里面的水，把壶扔在地上，径直离开。

女人怒火中烧，终于抑制不住怒气发作起来。她捡起地上的陶壶，用尽全力掷向那个男人。陶壶直接命中了男人后脑，碎成一片一片，男人也倒地昏迷流血不止。

女人怒气平息了，同时也意识到自己犯了一个多么大的错，她哭了起来。用公用电话叫了911，报告了这起事故。不久，一辆救护车和两辆警车来到现场。救护人员把男人抬上了担架，同时警察也拷上了那名男子的手脚。其中一个警察走到还在哭泣的女人身边说："这个城市欠你一声'谢谢'。那个人是一年多来我们最想抓到的罪犯，他是很多抢劫杀人案的主要犯罪嫌疑人。"

这个故事的寓意是我们无法简单得知的。我们总是愿意相信当我们完全摆脱内心的黑暗后我们能做出正确的选择，对我们自己和身边的人都有好处。但是生活并不是这样如同直线可以预测的。有时我们内心的黑暗会毫无预警地指引我们去做一些影响世界的积极的事，就像我们无条件的爱时常会让我们忽略那些发生在我们面前的罪恶。

从恶魔蜕变为天使需要花上多少时间呢，难道会是一瞬间？恶魔与天使的差距有多远呢，莫非就在一线之间？这或许是两个纠缠不清的问题，但我们都愿摒弃内心的恶魔，因为那代表着黑暗。我们欢迎天使的降临，因为即使我们不能永远地拥有光明，但是在追求光明的路上我们快乐比痛苦会更多一些。

53

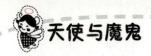

宽容天使篇
[之四]

Tolerance Is Gold

> The more we know, the better we forgive.
>
> 多一份理解，多一份宽容。

On August 23, 2004, the Athens Olympic horizontal bar final was going on vehemently (激烈地). Russian Nemov, 28, entered the arena third. He won the audience with the very difficult movement of rising high in the air and grabbing the bar, but when landing, he made a flaw, moving a step forward, so the referee only scored him 9.725 points.

At this moment, in the history of the Olympic Games, a rare instance appeared: the whole audience kept shouting "Nemov", "Nemov", and all rose, brandishing (挥舞) their arms and shooting their outrage to the referee long and loud. The competition was suspended. The fourth player, American Paul Ham, though ready, could only stand on the spot in embarrassment.

Faced with such a scenario (情景), Nemov who had withdrawn stood up from his seat, waved and greeted to the audience hailing him, bowed deeply and thanked them for their love and support. Nemov's magnanimity (宽宏大量) further kindled the audience's dissatisfaction. More boos rang while some of the audience even threw out their fists with thumbs down making indecent moves.

Against this enormous pressure, a referee was forced to score Nemov 9.762 points. However, such a score could not only appease (使平息) the audience's discontent, but boos sounded again.

54

Upon this, Nemov displayed his charisma and magnanimity. He returned to the game and raised his right arm to pay tribute to the audience and deeply bowed to express his gratitude. After that, he extended his right index finger to make a gesture for silence, and then pressed his hands down to request and soothe the audience to remain calm and give Paul Ham a quiet condition.

Nemov's tolerance set the interrupted game for over minutes going on.

In that game, Nemov didn't get a gold medal, but he was still a "champion" in the eyes of the audience; he didn't defeat the opponents, but he won the audience with his own tolerance.

When someone disagrees with you or offends you, don't lose your temper. Why? Because it is of no use to do so. You ought to be patient and keep calm lest you should quarrel with him. You must know that patience is not cowardice (怯懦), but a virtue. I hope that everybody practices it. In addition, patience will also bring us success. When you meet with difficulties in your work, it is also no use losing heart. You must keep on fighting till the final victory belongs to you.

Be kind. Everyone you meet is fighting a hard battle. The more we know, the better we forgive. Let us be slower to condemn and quicker to forgive. If we knew the other fellow's troubles, we might hesitate to criticize. We might admire his courage for carrying on. Go beyond yourself and reach out to other people with a sincere love, respect, caring and understanding of their needs. (471 words)

(Adapted from "Chicken Soup for the Soul")

宽容是金

2004年8月23日，雅典奥运会男子单杠决赛正在激烈进行。28岁的俄罗斯名将涅莫夫第三个出场。他以连续腾空抓杠的高难度动作征服了全场观众，但在落地时，他出现了一个小小的失误——向前移动了一步，裁判因此只给他打了9.725分。

此刻，奥运史上少有的情况出现了：全场观众不停地喊着"涅莫夫"、"涅莫夫"，而且全都站了起来，不停地挥舞着手臂，用持久而响亮的嘘声表达自己对裁判的愤怒。比赛被迫中断，第四个出场的美国选手保罗·哈姆虽已准备就绪，却只能尴尬地站在原地。

面对这种情景，已经退场的涅莫夫从座位上站起来，向朝他欢呼的观众挥手致意，并深深地鞠躬，感谢他们对自己的喜爱和支持。涅莫夫的大度进一步激发了观众的不满，嘘声更响了，一部分观众甚至伸出双拳，拇指朝下，做出不雅的动作。

面对如此大的压力，裁判被迫重新给涅莫夫打了9.762分。可是，这个分数不仅未能平息观众的不满，反而再次引起嘘声一片。

这时，涅莫夫显示出了他的人格魅力和宽广胸襟。他重新回到赛场，举起右臂向观众致意，深鞠一躬，表示感谢；接着，又伸出右手食指做出嘘声的手势，然后将双手下压，请求和劝慰观众保持冷静，给保罗·哈姆一个安静的比赛环境。

涅莫夫的宽容，让中断了十几分钟的比赛得以继续进行。

在那次比赛中，涅莫夫虽然没有拿到金牌，但他仍然是观众心目中的"冠军"；他没有打败对手，但他以自己的宽容征服了观众。

当有人和你意见不同或开罪于你的时候，不要发脾气。为什么？因为这样做无济于事。你应当忍耐并且保持冷静，避免和他争吵。你必须知道忍耐不是懦弱而是一种美德，我希望人人都这样做。另外，忍耐也会带给我们成功。你在工作中遭遇到困难的时候，灰心也毫无用处。你必须继续作战直到最后胜利属于你为止。

友善待人。你所遇到的每一个人都有自己的难处。多一份理解，多一份宽容。让我们在谴责前三思，多一些宽容。如果我们知道对方的烦恼，我们也许不会急于作出批评，我们也许会敬佩他坚持前进的勇气。超越自我，带着真诚的爱、尊重、关怀和对他人需求的理解向他人伸出援手。

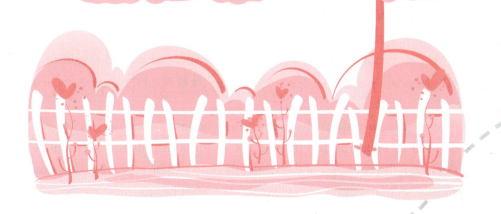

宽容不是懦弱，宽容是金子般熠熠生辉的美德。宽容不是一味的忍让，宽容天使引领我们进一步或退一步以便留一条出路给他人，如此，拥挤的道路通畅了，窘迫的境况化解了。不论谁比谁受益更多，毕竟难堪减少了，我们个人的价值与此同时得到了更加充分的发挥。

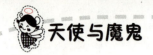

宽容天使篇

[之五]

To Leave the Grudge Behind

Forgiveness is a virtue of human beings.

原谅是人类的一种美德。

Mandela was put into prison for leading to fight against the whites' policy of apartheid (种族隔离). The white ruler imprisoned him in a deserted Ruben Island in the Atlantic Ocean for 27 years. At that time Mandela was already old, but the white ruler still cruelly maltreated him like a young prisoner.

Mandela was detained (扣押) in a "zinc-sheeted room" of the total concentration camp. In the daytime he smashed the large blocks into the stone stocks in the quarry. Sometimes he went into the icy sea to fish for kelp or mined the lime—every morning he lined up with the other prisoners to the quarry, and then was untied the fetters and dug the limestone with a sharp pick and shovel in the large quarry. Because he was an important criminal, Mandela had three guards altogether. They were not friendly, always finding various reasons to maltreat him.

No one imagined after he was out of prison and elected president in 1991, Mandela's action in his inauguration (就职典礼) shocked the whole world.

After the presidential inauguration began, Mandela got up and addressed to welcome the guests. He in turns introduced the political leaders from the countries of the world, then he said he was deeply honored to receive so many distinguished guests, but what he was most pleased was the three guards who guarded him first in Ruben Island prison also turned up. Immediately, he invited them to get up and introduced them to all the guests.

Mandela's open mind and spirit of tolerance made those white people who had cruelly maltreated him for 27 years ashamed while all the people present were filled with deep esteem. Watching the aged Mandela stood up slowly and respectfully saluted (敬礼) the three guards who had guarded him. All the guests present and the whole world calmed down.

Later, Mandela explained to his friends that when he was young, he was quick-tempered and irascible (易怒的). It was the life in prison that made him learn how to control his emotion, so he could survive. The years in prison gave him time and encouragement and made him learn how to deal with the pains he had encountered. He said that thanksgiving and tolerance often originate from the pain and tribulation (磨难), so we must train through the terribly strong willpower.

On the day he was released, he was calm, "When I walk out of the prison to the prison gate leading to freedom, I have made it clear that if I can't leave the grief and grudge behind, in fact I are still in prison."

Forgiveness is a virtue of human beings. It allows us to enjoy the warmth of the sunshine and can bridge the gap of human relationships. Forgiveness, which can be considered as patience and as a kind of self restrained behavior, is needed in every part of our lives. Forgiveness can also be regarded as a civilized behavior. It refers to a good way in which we sincerely and genuinely show politeness, kindness, friendship and respect to people. (502 words)

(Adapted from "Chicken Soup for the Soul")

把怨恨
留在身后

曼德拉因为领导反对白人的种族隔离政策而入狱。白人统治者把他关在荒凉的大西洋小岛罗本岛上达27年。当时曼德拉年事已高，但白人统治者依然像对待年轻犯人一样残酷虐待他。

曼德拉被关押在集中营一个"锌皮房"里。白天将采石场的大石块碎成石料。他有时要下到冰冷的海水里捞海带，有时干采石灰的活儿——每天早晨和其他犯人一起排队到采石场，然后被解开脚镣，在一个大采石场里用尖镐和铁锹挖石灰石。因为曼德拉是要犯，所以有三个看守。他们对他并不友好，总是找各种理由虐待他。

谁也没想到，1991年曼德拉出狱当选总统后，在就职典礼上的一个举动震惊了整个世界。

总统就职仪式开始后，曼德拉起身致词，欢迎来宾。他依次介绍了来自世界各国的政要，然后说，能接待这么多尊贵的客人，他深感荣幸，但他最高兴的是，当年在罗本岛监狱看守他的3名狱警也到场了。随即，他邀请他们起身，并把他们介绍给大家。

曼德拉的博大胸襟和宽容精神，令那些残酷虐待了他27年的白人汗颜，也让所有到场的人肃然起敬。看着年迈的曼德拉缓缓起身，恭敬地向三个关押他的看守致敬，在场的所有来宾乃至整个世界，都静了下来。

后来，曼德拉向朋友们解释说，自己年轻时急躁易怒，正是狱中生活使他学会了控制情绪，因此活了下来。牢狱岁月给了他时间和鼓励，也使他学会了如何处理自己遭遇的痛苦。他说，感恩与宽容常常源自痛苦与磨难，必须通过极强的毅力来训练。

获释当天，他心情平静："当我走出牢房，迈过通往自由的牢门时，我已经清楚，如果自己不能把悲痛与怨恨留在身后，那我其实仍在牢里。"

　　原谅是人类的一种美德。让我们感受到阳光般的温暖，沟通能消除人与人之间的隔阂。原谅被认为是一种耐性，同时它也是一种自律，世界的任何地方都需要它。原谅也是一种文明的举止，也是一种真诚地表示我们的礼貌、善良、友谊和尊敬的良好途径。

　　我们企盼宽容天使的降临，我们渴望感受到阳光般的温暖，而弥足珍贵的是，遭遇磨难时仍能心怀一份宽容，走出困境时却能抛弃怨恨，感恩磨难。宽容似乎有让冰雪消融的神奇力量，正如曼德拉所说，可贵的宽容源自痛苦与磨难，必须通过极强的毅力来训练。

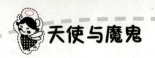

信心天使篇

[之一]

Attitude Is Everything

Each morning I wake up and say to myself, "Jerry, you have two choices today. You can choose to be in a good mood or you can choose to be in a bad mood." I choose to be in a good mood.

每天早上醒来我都告诉自己说："杰里，今天你有两个选择，你可以选择好心情，也可以选择坏心情。"我选择了好心情。

Jerry was always in a good mood and always had something positive (令人鼓舞的) to say. He was a unique manager because he had several waiters who had followed him around from restaurant to restaurant. The reason the waiters followed Jerry was because of his attitude.

One day I went up to Jerry and asked him, "I don't get it! You can't be a positive person all of the time. How do you do it?"

Jerry replied, "Each morning I wake up and say to myself, 'Jerry, you have two choices today. You can choose to be in a good mood or you can choose to be in a bad mood.' I choose to be in a good mood. Each time something bad happens, I can choose to be a victim (受害者) or I can choose to learn from it. I choose to learn from it. Every time someone comes to me complaining, I can choose to accept their complaining or I can point out the positive side of life. I choose the positive side of life."

Soon thereafter, I left the restaurant industry to start my own business. We lost touch, but I often thought about him.

Several years later, I heard that Jerry left the back door open one morning and was held up at by three armed robbers. While trying to open the safe, the robbers panicked (恐慌) and shot him.

Luckily, Jerry was found relatively quickly and rushed to the local trauma (创伤) center. After 18 hours of surgery and weeks of intensive care, Jerry was released from the hospital with fragments of the bullets still in his body.

I saw Jerry about six months after the accident. When I asked him how he was, he replied, "If I were any better, I'd be twins. Wanna see my scars?" I declined to see his wounds, but did ask him what had gone through his mind as the robbery took place.

"The first thing that went through my mind was that I should have locked the back door," Jerry replied. "Then, as I lay on the floor, I remembered that I had two choices: I could choose to live, or I could choose to die. I chose to live."

"Weren't you scared? Did you lose consciousness (意识)?" I asked.

Jerry continued, "The nurses kept telling me I was going to be fine. But when they wheeled (推动) me into the emergency room and I saw the expressions on the faces of the doctors and nurses, I got really scared. In their eyes, I read, 'He's a dead man.' I knew I needed to take action."

"When a nurse asked if I was allergic to anything. 'Yes,' I replied. The doctors and nurses stopped working as they waited for my reply. I took a deep breath and yelled, 'Bullets!'

Over their laughter, I told them, 'I am choosing to live. Operate on me as if I am alive, not dead.' "

Jerry lived thanks to the skill of his doctors, but also because of his amazing attitude.

Attitude, after all, is everything. (548 words)

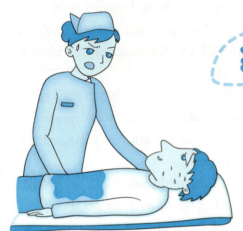

态度决定一切

杰里总是心情愉快、情绪高涨，说出积极的话来。他是个与众不同的经理，有好几个服务员都跟着他到不同的餐厅工作过。他们跟着杰里是因为他的生活态度。

有一天我走到杰里跟前问他："我不明白！你不可能事事都顺心。你是怎样做到一直都这么积极乐观的呢？"

杰里回答说："每天早上醒来后我对自己说，'杰里，今天你有两个选择。你可以选择好心情，也可以选择坏心情。'我选择了好心情。每次有坏事发生时，我可以选择成为受害者，也可以选择从中吸取教训，我选择了从中吸取教训。每当有人向我抱怨时，我可以选择听他们抱怨，或者给他们指出生活中积极的一面，我选择了指出生活中积极的一面。"

不久后，我离开餐饮业去追求个人发展。我们失去了联系，但我时常会想起杰里。

几年之后，我听说：一天早晨，杰里没关后门，三个持枪匪徒走进来，拿枪指着他。他们试图打开保险箱时，匪徒紧张之下开枪击中了他。

幸运的是，人们很远就发现了杰里，将他送到了当地的疗伤中心。经过18小时的手术和几星期的悉心护理，他终于出院了，体内还残留着子弹的碎片。

这事发生半年以后我见到了杰里。我问他身体怎样了，他答道："好极了！想不想看看我的伤疤？"我没看他的伤疤，但我问他抢劫案发生时，他在想什么。

杰里回答说："我首先想的是我要是把后门锁上就好了，但是躺在地板上的时候，我想到自己有两个选择：我可以选择生存，或是选择死亡。我选择了生存。"

"你难道一点也不怕吗？你失去知觉了吗？"我问。

杰里继续说："医生们很好，他们不断地告诉我没事。但他们推我进急救室时，我看到医生和护士脸上的表情，觉得很害怕。他们的眼睛里流露出'这个人要死了。'我知道我该采取些行动了。"

"当时有个护士问我对什么东西过敏吗，'有，'我回答说。医生和护士们都停下来等我回答。我深深吸了口气，喊道：'子弹！'

他们全笑起来，接着我对他们说：'我选择要活下来。给我动手术，把我当成个活人而不是死人来医治。'"

杰里活了下来，固然是因为医生的高超医术，但更主要是因为他那不屈不挠的态度。

毕竟，态度能决定一切。

美国教育家戴尔·卡耐尔在调查了很多名人的经历后指出："一个人事业上成功的因素，其中学识和专业技术只占15%，而良好的心理素质要占85%。"

信心对于立志成功者具有重要意义。它能够激发潜意识释放出无穷的热情、精力和智慧，进而帮助其获得巨大的财富与事业上的成就。

在生活上，如果缺少了自信心，在人生的大舞台上就施展不出自己的才华，表现不出自我。有多少人因为缺少自信而心灵上受到伤害，又有多少人因为缺少自信而错过了天赐的良机。相信自己，信心天使会帮助我们通往成功的阳光大道！

65

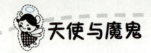

 信心天使篇
[之二]

Life Has the Time to Bloom

Give each grass the time to flower and give everyone a chance to prove his or her value. Don't blindly pull out a blade of grass or negate a person curtly and how many "rare orchids" we will get in our lives!

给每棵草开花的时间，给每个人以证明价值的机会。不要盲目地拔掉一株草，不要草率地否定一个人，那我们将会得到多少人生的"罕见的兰花"啊!

My friend went afar to work, so he asked me to take care of the courtyard in the mountains. The place adjacent (邻近的) to the wall was built with a fence to plant green vegetable. Every morning or evening, I would take a chair to sit in the courtyard sipping (啜饮) tea or reading. I felt it so charming.

My friend was an assiduous (勤奋的) man, so he often kept the courtyard clean and tidy without any weed. And I was so lazy, apart from occasionally sweeping the fallen leaves in the courtyard, that I never plucked (拔) grass shoots breaking through the earth, let them grow secretly. In the early spring, by the stone bench on the left side of the courtyard, sprouted (生长，发芽) several clusters (团) of buds, whose leaves were tender and flimsy. Over 20 days later, when their leaves unfurled (展开) richly, I discover they were like wild orchids (兰花) in the woods beyond the courtyard–if they were really the lingering wild orchids, it would be poetic with the quiet orchids wafting (飘荡) their fragrance gently.

In the later summer, the grass really bloomed. The little five-petal flowers steamed (产生气体) wisps of delicate fragrance. They shaped like those forest orchids, but they were wax yellow, unlike those forest wild orchids, whose flowers were purple or brown red. I picked one flower and some blades of grass, then came down the mountains to find a friend who collect and study plants. On seeing them, my friend immediately asked me where I picked them. After that, he congratulated (祝贺) on me, "You get rich!" I looked at my friend in puzzlement (困惑). He excitedly explained, "This is a strain (种类) of rare orchid, for many people are hard to find it in their lifetime. At the city flower market, this strain of orchid is worth at least 10,000 dollars each."

I called to tell the good news to the friend who had gone to work in the south. At this, my friend was stunned (震惊). After a while, he said gently, in fact, the orchid broke through the earth every year, but he thought it was an ordinary weed, so he often uprooted (连根拔起) it each spring it just sprouted. My friend couldn't help sighing, "I have almost destroyed a kind of rare flower; if I could wait for it to blossom with patience, it would have been discovered a few years before."

Yes, who will never miss some rare orchids in their own lives? We always plunk those wild weeds that haven't yet bloomed in time and don't give them the time to flower and bear fruit to prove their value.

Give each grass the time to flower and give everyone a chance to prove his or her value. Don't blindly pull out a blade of grass or negate a person curtly (粗率无礼地) and how many "rare orchids" we will get in our lives! (543 words)

(Extracted from "http://hi.baidu.com/taokuo103/blog/item/0eda09aef94d67044b36d684.html")

人生都有
开花的时候

朋友去远方工作，把他在山中的庭院交给我看管。院里临墙的地方扎了一道篱笆，种一些青菜。清晨或黄昏，我搬一把小椅子，坐在院里品茶读书，挺有韵味。

朋友是一个勤快人，院里常常收拾得干干净净寸草不生。而我很懒，除了偶尔扫扫院里的落叶，从不薅那些破土而出的草芽，任他们滋长。初春时，院子左侧的石凳旁冒出了几簇绿绿的牙尖，叶子又嫩又薄。20多天后，它们的叶子蓬蓬勃勃伸展开来，我才发觉像是院外林间幽幽的野兰——如果这是野兰，家有幽兰徐徐绽香，那该多富有诗意啊。

暮夏时，那株草果然开花了。五瓣小花氤氲着一缕缕幽香，花型如林中野兰一样，只是它是蜡黄的，不像林地里的那些紫色或褐红的野兰。我采集了一朵花和几片叶子，下山去找一位研究植物的朋友。朋友一看，忙问我这花在哪里采到的。之后，他恭贺我说："你发财了。"我不解望着朋友，他兴奋地解释说："这是一株稀有品种的兰花，许多人穷尽一生都很难找到它。如果在城市的花市上，这种兰花一株至少价值万余元。"

我打电话把喜讯告诉了远在南方的朋友。朋友一听，也愣了。过了一会儿，他轻轻地说，其实，那株兰花每年都要破土而出，只是他以为它是一株普通的野草，每年春天芽儿刚冒头就被他拔掉了。朋友不禁叹道："我几乎毁掉一种奇花啊，如果我能耐心地等它开花，几年前就能发现的。"

是的，我们谁又不曾错过人生中的那几株罕见的兰花呢？我们总是盲目地拔掉那些还没有来得及开花的野草，没有给它们开花结果证明自己价值的时间。

给每棵草开花的时间，给每个人以证明价值的机会，不要盲目地拔掉一株草，不要草率地否定一个人，那我们将会得到多少人生的"罕见的兰花"啊！

欣赏别人，是一种气度，一种发现，一种理解，一种智慧，一种境界。

美是到处都有的，对于眼睛，不是缺少美，而是缺少发现。懂得欣赏别人，才能更多地发现别人的优点，才能从他们身上汲取提升自己的能量。

给每棵草开花的时间，给每个人以证明价值的机会，不要盲目地拔掉一棵草，不要草率地否定一个人，那我们将会得到多少个人的"罕见的兰花"啊！

给自己一点时间，给自己一点信心，人生总有开花的时候。自信，便不会错过。

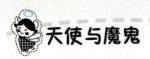

信心天使篇
[之三]
One Success Is Enough for Me!

People always complain about the bad weather. Actually the weather is not bad at all. As long as you are optimist and confident all the time, you will have a good weather everyday.

人们经常抱怨天气不好。实际上并不是天气不好。只要自己有乐观自信的心情，天天都是好天气。

There was a man who had undergone (经历) numerous failures in his life. But he said, "One success is enough for me!"

When he was five years old, his father died of illness without leaving him any property (财产). Since then, his mother worked outside while he had to stay at home and take care of his siblings (兄弟姐妹). He learnt cooking since then.

When he was fourteen, he dropped out from school and began his life of wandering.

When he was sixteen, he lied about his age to participate in the expedition (旅行). During the voyage, he was terribly seasick and sent back to his home ahead of time.

When he was eighteen, he married a girl, who, however, sold out all his properties and went back to her home several months after their marriage.

When he was twenty, he changed his job from electrician to ferry (运送) staff to railway worker. All his jobs were tough for him.

When he was thirty, he did sales work in an insurance company. But before long, he fell out with his boss due to the bonus problems.

When he was thirty—one, he learnt law by himself and began working in law with the encouragement of his friends. But in a trial, he fought with the litigant on court.

When he was thirty-two, he was out of work and led a tough life.

When he was thirty-five, misfortune (不幸) again befell (降临) on him. When he was driving across a huge bridge, the steel ropes along the edge of the bridge were broken and he fell into the river with his car. He suffered such severe injuries that he could no longer continue his job of promoting tires.

When he was forty, he opened a gas station in a town. However, he came into dispute because he beat his rivalries due to the billboard hanging problems.

When he was forty-seven, he divorced his second wife, which had deeply stricken his three children.

When he was sixty-one, he campaigned for a senator but failed at last.

When he was sixty-five, his on-growth restaurant was dismantled by the government. He was compelled to sell out all his facilities at a very low price.

When he was sixty-six, he made a living by promoting his chicken-frying technics to various restaurants in different places.

When he was seventy-five, he felt powerless to maintain his company, so he transferred his brand and patent to others. The new owner suggested giving him ten thousand stock shares as part of the purchasing price. But he turned down the suggestion. Later the price of the stocks of the company soared and he lost the chance of being a billionaire.

When he was eighty-three, he opened another fast-food restaurant but fell into a lawsuit due to trademark and patent issues.

When he was eighty-eight, he achieved great success and became well-known to the whole world.

He was exactly the founder of Kentucky Fried Chicken, Ha Lunde Sandoz. He often said, "People always complain about the bad weather. Actually the weather is not bad at all. As long as you are optimist and confident all the time, you will have a good weather everyday." (557 words)

成功一次就够了!

有一个人，一生中经历了无数失败。但他却说："成功一次就够了!"

5岁时，他的父亲突然病逝，没有留下任何财产，母亲外出做工。年幼的他在家照顾弟妹，并学会自己做饭。

14岁时，他辍学离校，开始了流浪生活。

16岁时，他谎报年龄参加了远征军。因航行途中晕船厉害，被提前遣送回乡。

18岁时，他娶妻结婚。但只过了几个月，妻子就变卖了他所有的财产逃回娘家。

20岁时，他当电工、开轮渡，后来又当铁路工人，没有一样工作顺利。

30岁时，他在保险公司从事推销工作，后因奖金问题与老板闹翻而辞职。

31岁时，他自学法律，并在朋友的鼓动下当起了律师。一次审案时，竟在法庭上与当事人大打出手。

32岁时，他失业了，生活非常艰难。

35岁时，不幸再次降临到他的头上。当他开车路过一座大桥时，大桥钢绳断裂。他连人带车跌到河中，身受重伤，无法再干轮胎推销员工作。

40岁时，他在一个镇上开了一家加油站，因挂广告牌问题把竞争对手打伤，引来一场纠纷。

47岁时，他与第二任妻子离婚，三个孩子深受打击。

61岁时，他竞选参议员，但最后落败。

65岁时，政府修路拆了他刚刚红火的快餐馆，他不得不低价出售了所有设备。

66岁时，为了维持生活，他到各地的小餐馆推销自己掌握的炸鸡技术。

75岁时，他感到力不从心，转让了自己创立的品牌和专利。新主人提议给他1万股，作为购买价的一部分，他拒绝了。后来公司股票大涨，他因此失去了成为亿万富翁的机会。

83岁时，他又开了一家快餐店，却因商标专利与人打起了官司。

88岁时，他终于大获成功，全世界都知道了他的名字。

他，就是肯德基的创始人——哈伦德·山德士。他说："人们经常抱怨天气不好。实际上并不是天气不好。只要自己有乐观自信的心情，天天都是好天气。"

积极乐观的情绪状态，会使人心情愉悦、精神高昂、精力充沛，对生活充满热情与信心。因此，生活中，我们应学会自我调控情绪，排除不良情绪，即使走进困境，也要抱着"山重水复疑无路，柳暗花明又一村"的乐观心态，这样才能让自己在愉快的环境中度过每一天。

乐观是心胸豁达的表现，乐观是生理健康的目的，乐观是人际交往的基础，乐观是工作顺利的保证，乐观是避免挫折的法宝，也为我们的信心天使插上了翅膀！

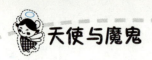

信心天使篇

[之四]

Look out, Baby, I Am Your Love Man

> Because of his preparation, Les was ready. He vowed the audience and his general manager. From that fateful beginning, Les went on to a successful career in broadcasting, politics, public speaking and television.
>
> 有了精心准备，莱斯才能如此从容。他赢得了听众和总经理的心。从那改变一生的机遇起，莱斯开始了在广播、政治、演讲和电视等方面的成功的职业生涯。

Les Brown and his twin brother were adopted by Mamie Brown, a kitchen worker and maid, shortly after their birth in a poverty-stricken (极度贫穷的) Miami neighborhood.

Because of his hyperactivity (好动) and nonstop jabber (含糊说话), Les was placed in special education classes for the learning disabled in grade school and throughout high school. Upon graduation, he became a city sanitation (公共卫生) worker in Miami Beach. But he had a dream of being a disc jockey.

At night he would take a transistor radio to bed where he listened to the local radio. He created an imaginary radio station in his tiny room with its torn flooring. A hairbrush (梳子) served as his microphone as he practiced his patter, introducing records to his ghost listeners.

His mother and brother could hear him through the thin walls and would shout at him to quit flapping (轻拍) his jaws and go to sleep. But Les didn't listen to them. He was wrapped (包裹) up in his own world, living a dream.

One day Les boldly went to the local radio station during his lunch break from mowing (割草) grass for the city. He got into the station manager's office and told him he wanted to be a disc jockey.

And so Les returned to the station every day for a week, asking if there were any job openings. Finally the station manager gave in and took him on as an errand boy with no pay. At first, he fetched coffee or picked up lunches and dinners for the deejays who could not leave the studio. Eventually his enthusiasm (热情) for their work won him the confidence of the disc jockeys who would send him in their Cadillacs to pick up visiting celebrities.

One Saturday afternoon while Les was at the station, a deejay named Rock was drinking while on the air.

Mr. Klein,the station manager then asked, "Young man, do you know how to work the controls in the studio?"

"Yes sir," replied Les.

Les darted (急冲) into the booth, gently moved Rock aside and sat down at the turntable. He was ready. And he was hungry. He flipped on the microphone switch and said, "Look out! This is me LB, triple P–Les Brown, Your Platter Playing Poppa. There were none before me and there will be none after me. Therefore, that makes me the one and only. Young and single and love to mingle. Certified (注意), bona fide(宝贝), qualified (合格的) to bring you satisfaction, a whole lot of action. Look out, baby, I'm your love man."

Because of his preparation, Les was ready. He vowed the audience and his general manager. From that fateful beginning, Les went on to a successful career in broadcasting, politics, public speaking and television. (506 words)

(Extracted from "http://www.zk168.com.cn/sanwen/yingyu_93040.html")

注意了，宝贝，我就是你们最喜爱的人！

莱斯·布朗和他的双胞胎兄弟出生在迈阿密一个非常贫困的社区，出生后不久就被帮厨女工梅米·布朗收养了。

莱斯非常好动，又含含糊糊地说个不停，所以他小学就被安排进一个专门为学习有障碍的学生开设的特教班，直到高中毕业。毕业后，成了迈阿密滩的一名城市环卫工人。但他却一直梦想成为一名电台音乐节目主持人。

每天晚上，他都要把晶体管收音机抱到床上，听本地电台节目。就在他那间狭小的、铺着破损的地板革的房间里，他创建了一个假想的电台——用一把梳子当麦克风，他念经一般喋喋不休地练习向他的"影子"听众介绍唱片。

透过薄薄的墙壁，他母亲和兄弟都能听到他的声音，并且对他大喊大叫，让他别再耍嘴皮子早点睡觉。但是，莱斯根本就不理睬他们，他已经完全沉醉在自己的世界里，努力想要实现他的梦想。

一天，莱斯利用在市区割草的午休时间，勇敢地来到了本地电台。他走进经理办公室，告诉他自己想成为一名流行音乐节目主持人。

此后莱斯连续一周天天都来这家电台，询问是否有职位空缺。最后，电台经理终于让步了，决定雇他跑腿打杂，但没有薪水。刚开始时，莱斯的工作是为那些不能离开播音室的主持人们取咖啡或者是去买午餐和晚餐。由于莱斯对工作积极热情，终于赢得了音乐节目主持人的信任，让他开着主持人的卡迪拉克车去接电台邀请来的一些名人。

一个星期六的下午，莱斯还在电台，主持人罗克边播音边喝着酒。

电台经理克莱恩先生问道："年轻人，你知道在演播室如何让这些控制器工作吗？"

"是的，先生！"莱斯答道。

莱斯箭一般地冲进演播室，轻轻地把罗克移到一边，坐在了录音转播台前。他准备好了！而且早就渴望这个机会来临。他轻轻打开麦克风开关，说："注意了！我是莱斯·布朗，人称唱片播放大叔，可以说是前无古人，后无来者，因此，我是举世无双，天下惟一。我年纪轻轻，单身一人，喜欢和大家在一起倾听音乐，品味生活。我的能力是经过鉴定的，绝对真实可靠，一定能够带给你们一档丰富多彩的节目，让你们满意。注意了，宝贝，我就是你们最喜爱的人。"

有了精心准备，莱斯才能如此从容。他赢得了听众和总经理的心！从那改变一生的机遇起，莱斯开始了在广播、政治、演讲和电视等方面的成功的职业生涯。

爱默生曾说过：自信是成功的第一秘诀。自信是人对自身力量的一种肯定，深信自己，便能使之成为指引你走向成功目标的一种信念。正如莱斯一样，拥有信心，便可以化渺小为伟大，化平庸为神奇。平凡的人也会因自信而创造出惊人的事业。以自信提升成功的几率，以成功增加自信的砝码，这就是自信者的人生！

77

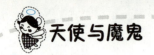

 信心天使篇

[之五]

A Girl Named Lille

Well, if she thinks it's good, then it must be good. I think I'll stay!

如果她觉得我做得很棒，那么我一定是真的做得很棒。我想我会被留下的！

Lille was a young French Canadian girl. At the age of 16, she was forced to drop out of school to contribute to the family income. In 1922, with English as her second language and limited education and skills, the future didn't look bright for Lille.

Her father was a stern (严格的) man. He demanded that Lille find a job. But her limitations left her with little confidence and low self-esteem (自尊), and she didn't know what work she could do.

With small hope of gaining employment, she would still ride the bus daily into the "big cities". But she couldn't muster (集合) the courage to respond to a Help Wanted ad; she couldn't even bring herself to knock on a door. Her father would ask, "Any luck today, Lille?" "No, no luck today, Dad," she would respond meekly (温顺地). As the days passed, the questions became more demanding, and Lille knew she would soon have to knock on a door.

On one of her trips, Lille saw a sign at the Carhartt Overall Company. "Help Wanted," the sign said, "Secretarial. Apply Within." She walked up the long flight of stairs to the Company offices. Cautiously (谨慎地), Lille knocked on her very first door. She was met by the office manager, Margaret Costello. In her broken English, Lille told her she was interested in the secretarial position, falsely (错误地) stating that she was 19. Margaret knew something wasn't right, but decided to give the girl a chance. She guided Lille through the old business office of the Company. With rows and rows of people seated at rows and rows of typewriters and adding machines, Lille felt as if a hundred pairs of eyes were staring at her. With her chin on her chest and her eyes staring down, the reluctant (不情愿的) girl followed Margaret to the back of the room.

Margaret sat her down at a typewriter and said, "Lille, let's see how good you really are." On her first try, Lille got through one line. It had five words, and she made four mistakes. On her second attempt, Lille got through a full paragraph, but still made many mistakes. She pulled out the paper, threw it out and started over. This time she completed the letter, but her work was still strewn (散布于) with errors. She looked at the clock: 11:55—five minutes to freedom.

Just then, the door at one end of the office opened and Margaret walked in. She came directly over to Lille. She read the letter and paused. Then she said, "Lille, you're doing good work!"

Lille was stunned. She looked at the letter, then up at Margaret. With those simple words of encouragement, her desire to escape vanished and her confidence began to grow. She thought, "Well, if she thinks it's good, then it must be good. I think I'll stay!"

Lille did stay at the Company for 51 years, all because someone had the insight (洞察力) to give a shy and uncertain young girl the gift of self-esteem when she knocked on the door.(537 words)

有个女孩叫莉儿

莉儿是个年轻的法裔加拿大女孩。16岁那年，她被迫辍学挣钱，贴补家用。那是1922年，对于一个英语是第二外语，而所受的教育和培训又有限的女孩来说，莉儿看起来前途渺茫。

她的父亲非常严厉，要莉儿找份工作。然而，因为条件有限，莉儿没有一点儿自信，她很自卑，不知道自己能干点什么。

虽然就业机会渺茫，可莉儿仍然每天搭公车到那些"大城市"去。但是她鼓不起勇气去应聘那些广告上的职位，甚至连敲门的信心都没有。父亲总是问："今天运气怎么样，莉儿？""今天运气不好，爸爸。"她嗫嚅着回答。日子一天天过去，父亲的问题变得越来越苛严，莉儿知道她必须马上敲开一家公司的门。

这天，在底特律市中心的卡哈特服装公司，莉儿看到这样一则招聘告示："招聘文秘，应聘者请进。"莉儿踏上了通往卡哈特公司办公室的长长楼梯，她生平第一次小心翼翼地扣响了一扇陌生的门。接待她的是办公室经理玛格丽特·科斯特洛。莉儿结结巴巴地用英语说对那个秘书职位很感兴趣，并谎称自己已经19岁了。玛格丽特知道她说的不全是真话，但还是决定给她一次机会。她带莉儿穿过卡哈特公司那间陈旧的办公室，里面有一排排的人，坐在一排排的打字机、计算器前面，莉儿觉得仿佛有一百双眼睛正盯着自己。她害羞得下巴抵到了胸前，两眼盯着地面，不情愿地跟着玛格丽特来到那间办公室后排。

玛格丽特安排她坐到一台打字机前，对她说："莉儿，让我们见识一下你的真本事吧。"第一次，莉儿打了一行，五个单词，她打错了四个。第二次，她打了一段，但还是打错了很多地方。她把那张纸抽出来扔掉，然后重新开始。这次她把信打完了，可还是满篇错误。她看看钟：11:55，再过五分钟就解放了。

这时，办公室另一端的门开了，玛格丽特走了进来。她径直走到莉儿跟前，读着那封信，然后停下来对莉儿说："莉儿，你做得很棒！"

莉儿极为震惊。她看看信，又抬头看看玛格丽特。正是这么简短的一句鼓励话打消了莉儿逃跑退缩的念头，让她鼓起了信心。她想："如果她觉得我做得很棒，那么我一定是真的做得很棒。我想我会被留下的！"

莉儿确实留了下来，而且在这家公司一待就是51年。而她之所以能做到这一切，完全是因为曾有一个人在当初那个羞怯的小女孩敲门的一刻给了她自尊自信。

现实中的恐惧，远比不上想象中那么可怕。所以敢于面对挑战，鼓起勇气，敢于尝试，你的自信就会慢慢高涨起来。

自信地朝着理想中的目标前进，过你想过的生活。随着自信的激励，人生的法则也会变得简单，孤独将不再孤独，贫穷将不再贫穷，脆弱将不再脆弱！因为自信天使会永远住在我们的心中！

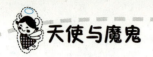

执着天使篇
[之一]
I'll Always Be There for You!

No matter what happens, I'll always be there for you!

不管发生什么，我永远都会在你的身边！

In 1989, an 8.2 earthquake almost flattened (夷为平地) America, killing over 30,000 people in less than four minutes. In the midst of utter devastation (毁灭) and chaos (混乱), a father left his wife safely at home and rushed to the school where his son was supposed to be, only to discover that the building was as flat as a pancake.

After the unforgettably initial shock, he remembered the promise he had made to his son: "No matter what, I'll always be there for you!" And tears began to fill his eyes. As he looked at the pile of ruins that once was the school, it looked hopeless, but he kept remembering his commitment (承诺) to his son.

He began to direct his attention towards where he walked his son to class at school each morning. Remembering his son's classroom would be in the back right corner of the building, he rushed there and started digging through the ruins.

As he was digging, other helpless parents arrived, clutching their hearts (揪心), saying: "My son!" "My daughter!" Other well-meaning parents tried to pull him off what was left of the school, saying: "It's too late! They're all dead! You can't help! Go home! Come on, face reality, there's nothing you can do!"

To each parent he responded with one line: "Are you going to help me now?" And then he continued to dig for his son, stone by stone. The fire chief showed up and tried to pull him off the school's ruins saying, "Fires are breaking out, and explosions are happening everywhere. You are in danger. We'll take care of it. Go home." To which this loving, caring American father asked, "Are you going to help me now?"

The police came and said, "You're angry, anxious and it's over. You're endangering others. Go home. We'll handle it!" To which he replied, "Are you going to help me now?" No one helped.

Courageously he went on alone because he needed to know for himself: "Is my boy alive or is he dead?" He dug for 8 hours... 12 hours... 24 hours... 36 hours... then, in the 38th hour, he pulled back a large stone and heard his son's voice. He screamed his son's name, "ARMAND!" He heard back, "Dad!?! It's me, Dad! I told the other kids not to worry. I told them that if you were alive, you'd save me and when you saved me, they'd be saved. You promised, 'No matter what happens, I'll always be there for you!' You did it, Dad!" "What's going on in there? How is it?" the father asked.

"There are 14 of us left out of 33, Dad. We're scared, hungry, thirsty and thankful you're here. When the building collapsed, it made a triangle, and it saved us."

"Come out, boy!"

"No, Dad! Let the other kids out first, cause I know you'll get me! No matter what happens, I know you'll always be there for me!" (504 words)

(Extracted from "Chicken Soup for the Soul")

我永远都会在你的身边!

1989年,一次8.2级的地震几乎铲平美国,在短短不到4分钟的时间里,夺去了3万多人的生命。在一片瓦砾和混乱之中,一位父亲将他的妻子在家里安顿好后,赶到他儿子就读的学校,却看到校园已被夷为平地。

看到这令人震惊的一幕,他想起了曾经对儿子所作的承诺:"不论发生什么事,我永远都会在你的身边!"至此,父亲热泪盈眶。目睹曾经的学校成为了一片废墟,真叫人绝望。但父亲的脑中仍然牢记着他对儿子的诺言。

他开始努力回忆每天早上送儿子上学的必经之路。终于记起儿子的教室应该就在那幢建筑物后面,位于右边的角落里,他跑到那儿,开始在碎石砾中挖掘。

这位父亲正在挖掘时,其他束手无策的学生家长赶到现场,揪心地叫着:"我的儿子呀!""我的女儿呀!"一些好意的家长试图劝说这位父亲离开现场,告诉他:"一切都太迟了!他们全死了!这样做没用的,回去吧!面对现实,你无能为力了!"。

面对种种劝告,这位父亲的回答只有一句话:"你们愿意帮我吗?"然后继续进行挖掘工作,在废墟中寻找他的儿子。消防队长出现了,他也试图把这位父亲劝走,对他说:"火灾频现,四处都在发生爆炸,你在这里太危险了,这边的事我们会处理,你回家吧!"对此,这位慈爱、关切的父亲仍然回答:"你们能帮我吗?"

警察赶到现场,对他说:"你现在又气又急,该结束了。你在危及他人,回家吧!我们会处理一切的。"这位父亲依旧回答:"你们愿意帮我吗?"然而,人们无动于衷。

为了弄清楚儿子是死是活，这位父亲独自一人鼓起勇气，继续挖掘。他挖了8小时……12小时……24小时……36小时……38小时后，父亲推开了一块巨大的石头，听到了儿子的声音。父亲尖叫着："阿曼德！"他听到了儿子的回音："爸爸吗？是我，爸爸，我告诉其他的小朋友不要着急。我告诉他们如果你活着，你会来救我的。如果我得救了，他们也就得救了。你答应过我，'不论发生什么，我永远都会在你的身边！'你做到了，爸爸！""你那里的情况怎样？"父亲问。

"我们有33个同学，只有14个活着。爸爸，我们好害怕，又渴又饿，谢天谢地，你在这儿。教室倒塌时，刚好形成一个三角形的洞，救了我们。"

"快出来吧，儿子!"

"不，爸！让其他小朋友先出来吧！因为我知道你会接我的!不管发生什么事，我知道你永远都会来到我的身边！"

"不管发生什么，我永远都会在你的身边!"这是一位父亲对自己的孩子说过的一句话。然而这不只是简单的一句话，而是一个承诺，也是身陷险境中的孩子求生的希望和信念。同时也是父亲的顽强、执着挽救了14个孩子宝贵的生命。

百慕达奶油花的花语之一是顽强、执着，让我们感谢这位头戴奶油花的执着天使。同时也让这位美丽的天使住进我们心中。

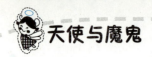

 执着天使篇
[之二]

Surgeon Benjamin Carson

Today Benjamin Carson, the boy who thought he was the dumbest boy in his 5th grade class, is a world famous surgeon at the prestigious Johns Hopkins Hospital in Maryland.

如今曾经被视作五年级最笨的学生本杰明·卡森成了马里兰州约翰·霍普金斯医院世界知名的外科医生。

In the Fifth grade, Benjamin Carson thought he was one of the dumbest (愚蠢的) kids in his class. His classmates thought he was one of the dumbest, his teacher thought he was one of the dumbest, and he thought he was one of the dumbest. Therefore, when he brought home a report that poor progress, Benjamin was very philosophical (达观的) about it. He told his mother, "Yah, you know it doesn't matter very much."

His mother was a different opinion. Having only a third grade education, Mrs. Carson knew that her children's only chance to escape poverty was through a good education. Her two boys were not reaching their potential at school, and she knew that if they were going to get a good education, it would have to start at home. She began with three rules. Rule number one, the boys would only be allowed to watch two pre-selected TV shows per week. Rule number two, the two boys would have to finish all their homework before they could watch TV or even play outside. Rule number three, the boys would have to read two books from the library each week and write a book report on each of them.

Benjamin was dismay (沮丧) at these new rules and tried very hard to talk his mother out of them. She stood firm, and not thinking to disobey (违抗) his mother, he followed her rules. Before long he saw the fruits of his

labor, when he was the only one who knew an answer to a question the teacher asked the class. Then there was a second question only he knew the answer to. His teacher and rest of his classmates were surprised that he knew the correct answer to such hard questions. He was even a little surprised himself, but he knew his knowledge came from the books he was reading. He began to surmise (猜测) that if he could learn just more facts from books at the library he could learn anything.

Benjamin continued on his road of growth and became an academic leader in his school. He had learned to love reading and realized that he could channel (引导) that love into learning. He did not care jeers (嘲笑) of others. Mrs. Carson demanded that they take their education seriously and gave them a structure way they could do it. Today Benjamin Carson, the boy who thought he was the dumbest boy in his 5th grade class, is a world famous surgeon (外科医生) at the prestigious (有声望的) Johns Hopkins Hospital in Maryland. (456 words)

(Extracted from "http://www.resilienceproject.com/stories4.html")

外科医生
本杰明·卡森

五年级的本杰明·卡森认为自己是班里最笨的学生之一，同学们都认为他是最笨的，他的老师也这样认为，他自己也有同感。所以，每次他拿回家很差的成绩报告时，本杰明都非常达观。他告诉妈妈："是呀，你知道没关系。"

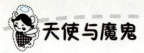

天使与魔鬼

他的妈妈却不这样认为，虽然妈妈只有三年级的教育，卡森夫人知道孩子摆脱贫困惟一的机会就是通过良好的教育。他的两个儿子在学校没有发挥自己的潜力，她知道如果他们能够有良好的教育必须首先从家里开始。她订立了三个原则。第一，孩子们每周只能看两个预先选好的电视节目。第二，两个孩子只有完成作业后才能看电视或出去玩。第三，孩子们每周都要读图书馆里两本书，写读书报告。

本杰明对这些新规定非常沮丧，试图劝妈妈不要这样做，但是妈妈态度很坚定。他不敢违抗妈妈，遵循了她的规定。不久他就看到了自己努力的成果，老师提问每个同学问题时，只有他能回答上来。他的老师和其他同学们都很吃惊这么难的问题他都知道答案。他自己也很吃惊，但是他知道自己的知识都是从书中阅读而来。他开始猜测是否可以从图书馆里学习更多的知识。

本杰明继续长大成了学校里学习最棒的人。他开始喜爱阅读并且意识到将对阅读的热爱转移到学习中，不理会别人的嘲笑。他的母亲要求孩子们好好学习，教给他们正确的方法。如今曾经被视作五年级最笨的学生本杰民·卡森成了马里兰州约翰·霍普金斯医院世界知名的外科医生。

在走向成功的路上，有些人是幸运的，他们总可以比别人走得更快、更远，做得更好、更高。但同时他们也具有异于他人的优秀品质——坚毅与执着。执着就是一种不放弃的精神，是对事业、前途、生活目标不懈地追求。一个人的精力有限，时间有限，在有生之年，只有把握住自己真正的志趣与才能所在，专一地做下去，才可能有所成就，得到执着天使的垂青。

执着天使篇
[之三]
Power of Persistence

The Brooklyn Bridge shows us that dreams that seem impossible can be realized with determination and persistence, no matter what the odds are.

布鲁克林大桥的故事告诉我们不管困难是什么，依靠决心和坚持看似不可能的梦想就可能实现。

In 1883, a creative engineer named John Roebling was inspired by an idea to build a spectacular bridge connecting New York with the Long Island. However, bridge building experts throughout the world thought that this was an impossible feat and told Roebling to forget the idea. It just could not be done. It was not practical. It had never been done before.

Roebling could not ignore the vision he had in his mind of this bridge. He thought about it all the time and he knew deep in his heart that it could be done. He just had to share the dream with someone else. After much discussion and persuasion he managed to convince his son Washington, an engineer, that the bridge in fact could be built.

The project started well, but when it was only a few months underway a tragic accident on the site took the life of John Roebling. Washington was injured and left with a certain amount of brain damage, which resulted in him not being able to walk or talk or even move.

Everyone had a negative comment to make and felt that the project should be scrapped since the Roeblings were the only ones who knew how the bridge could be built. In spite of his handicap, Washington was never

89

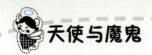
discouraged and still had a burning desire to complete the bridge and his mind was still as sharp as ever.

As he lay on his bed in his hospital room, with the sunlight streaming through the windows, a gentle breeze blew the flimsy white curtains apart and he was able to see the sky and the tops of the trees outside for just a moment. It seemed that there was a message for him not to give up. Suddenly an idea hit him. All he could do was move one finger and he decided to make the best use of it. By moving this, he slowly developed a code of communication with his wife.

He touched his wife's arm with that finger, indicating to her that he wanted her to call the engineers again. Then he used the same method of tapping (轻敲) her arm to tell the engineers what to do. It seemed foolish but the project was under way again.

For 13 years Washington tapped out his instructions with his finger on his wife's arm, until the bridge was finally completed. Today the spectacular Brooklyn Bridge stands in all its glory as a tribute to the triumph of one man's indomitable spirit and his determination not to be defeated by circumstances. It is also a tribute to the engineers and their team work, and to their faith in a man who was considered mad by half the world. It stands too as a tangible monument to the love and devotion of his wife who for 13 long years patiently decoded the messages of her husband and told the engineers what to do.

Often when we face obstacles in our day-to-day life, our hurdles (障碍) seem very small in comparison to what many others have to face. The Brooklyn Bridge shows us that dreams that seem impossible can be realized with determination and persistence, no matter what the odds are. (543 words)

(Extracted from "http://www.indianchild.com/inspiring_stories.htm")

坚持的力量

1883年，一位富于创新精神的建筑师约翰·罗布林想要建一座连接纽约与长岛城的大桥，可是全球所有的桥梁专家都认为这是不可能的事情，并且告诉罗布林打消这个念头，这是一项根本无法实现的工程。它不切实际，以前从来没有人做过。

罗布林不想放弃自己的计划，他每时每刻都在筹划着，深信桥一定会建成。他要让人分享他的梦想。经过无数次的讨论与劝说，他成功说服了自己的工程师儿子华盛顿，相信大桥一定能建成。

开始时这项工程一切都很顺利，但几个月以后，约翰·罗布林在一场突如其来的工地悲剧事故中不幸身亡，华盛顿也受了伤。由于头部受伤的后遗症，他无法走路、说话、行动。

每个人都对这个项目持否定态度，感到应该废弃这个项目，因为只有罗布林父子知道怎么建桥。华盛顿不顾自己身体的不便，强烈地想要完成这座桥，他的大脑仍然和以前一样聪敏。

他躺在医院的病床上，阳光穿过窗户，一阵清风吹过轻薄的白色窗帘，偶尔他能够看到蓝天和树顶。似乎有一个信息告诉他不要放弃。突然他想到了一个主意，他所能做的只是能动一个手指，他决心要好好利用它。慢慢地他摸索出了通过动这个手指和妻子交流的方法。

他用自己的手指摸着妻子的胳膊，指示她想和其他工程师再次联系。然后他用同样的方法轻轻敲着妻子的胳膊告诉工程师怎样做。看起来似乎很愚蠢，但是工程再次开始了。

整整13年华盛顿用自己的手指轻轻敲着妻子的胳膊作出指示，直到建成这座大桥。如今壮观的布鲁克林大桥成为不屈不挠的精神和永不言败的决心的标志。这也是所有工程师精诚合作，坚信一个很多人认为是疯狂的

91

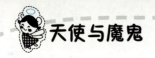

信念的结果。也是妻子爱和奉献的丰碑，是妻子十三年来耐心解读丈夫信息从而告诉工程师如何操作的结果。

当我们面对平常生活的障碍，我们的困难与很多其他人的困难相比似乎非常渺小。布鲁克林大桥的故事告诉我们不管困难是什么，依靠决心和坚持，看似不可能的梦想就可能实现。

河蚌忍受了沙粒的磨砺，坚持不懈，终于孕育绝美的珍珠；顽铁忍受了烈火的赤炼，坚持不懈，终于炼成锋利的宝剑。一切豪言壮语皆是虚幻，惟有坚定的信念才是踏向成功的基石。

生命的奖赏远在旅途终点，而非起点附近。不知道要走多少步才能达到目标。踏上第一千步的时候，仍然可能遭到失败。但成功就藏在拐角后面，除非拐了弯，我们永远不知道还有多远。

坚持梦想，努力拼搏，才能扬起梦想的风帆，在大海上乘风破浪。就像贝多芬时时听见命运的敲门声；就像爱迪生刻刻点亮人生的明灯；像莱特兄弟，相信自己会飞，就一定能翱翔在蓝天之上，找到自己的执着天使。

执着天使篇

[之四]

The Shortest Fireman

I just set my mind to something and I go out and do my best.

我下定决心做某件事情，就会全力以赴。

Training to be a fireman is a tough thing for anyone, but obstacle is bigger when you're 4 feet 2 inches tall.

Still, Vince Brasco, 19, hasn't let a little thing like height stop him from volunteering at his local fire department in Carbon, Pennsylvania, for the past four years, despite being born with a type of dwarfism (侏儒症) that affects bone growth.

"I'll never let having dwarfism stop me from doing anything. I just set my mind to something and I go out and do my best. I wanted to be a fireman as a child so as soon as I was old enough to volunteer at 16. I did it."

Dwarfism is a disability (残疾), but it hasn't affected Brasco's ability from going full blaze (烈火) when it comes to fighting fires. He races to emergencies (紧急情况) up to three times a day along with the rest of his crew (工作人员), who are all much higher than him. In fact, when there's a big fire, Brasco operates the hose (橡皮软管) at neighborhood blazes with his colleagues, helping to control the high-pressure jets (高压水流喷射).

A painful knee and various medical problems have required him to have 14 surgeries (外科手术) on his left leg. But that hasn't prevented him

93

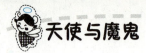

from doing the job.

Brasco says the doctor who gave him the physical exam to join the fire squad (小组) tried to talk him out of it. "It was a pretty heated argument because he doesn't know me. He doesn't know what I can do. I'm just like everyone else. I just do things a little different. It's just different things I might need help with. I'm not afraid to ask for help."

Although Brasco is only 87 pounds, he can lift barbell (杠铃) of 265 pounds, which he says is necessary to handle the hoses and other heavy-duty equipment. "I work out a lot -- as much as I can down at my gym. It really helps on the job. We need to be strong. Because I can lift so much, I'm handy at salvage (救援) jobs where we have to move heavy bits of metal debris (残骸)-- like after car accidents."

When there is a fire going, Brasco wears a custom-made (定制的) fire suit while on the job. "We had to take a normal suit and have it reduced down to fit me. It was great when I put it on for the first time."

While Brasco isn't fighting fires, he works part time at his local Best Buy and is studying to become a nurse to help others with health needs. But whenever he can, he responds to the calls for the volunteer fire service. "If I am in the area, then I just drop everything and run."

Brasco hopes that once he completes his Firefighter Essentials exam, he'll be allowed to enter burning buildings. "Until then, I'm happy to just fight fires from the outside, and attend other emergencies, but I know I've got what it takes." (546 words)

(Extracted from "http://www.hjenglish.com/new/p231087/")

最矮的消防员

想成为一名消防员，对任何人来说都不是件容易的事情，尤其是当你的身高只有4英尺2英寸。

然而，19岁的文思·布拉斯科却没让身高这样的小事，阻止他成为宾夕法尼亚州卡本市消防部门的一名志愿者。尽管出生时患有一种影响骨头生长的侏儒症，现在他已经在消防部门里工作了四年。

"我绝不会让侏儒症阻止我做任何事情。我下定决心做某件事情，就会全力以赴。我很小就梦想成为一名消防员，16岁就成了消防志愿者，实现了我的梦想。"

侏儒症是一种残疾，但这并不影响布拉斯科灭火的能力。他和同事们有时一天三次冲向紧急情况现场。当然了，他的所有同事都比他高一大截。事实上，当有大火发生时，布拉斯科会和他的同事在火场外操作水枪，帮助控制高压水流的喷射。

由于疼痛的膝盖和各种健康问题，他不得不在左腿上做了14次手术。但那并没有妨碍他的工作。

布拉斯科说，他加入消防队时，体检的医生劝说他不要当消防员。"由于他不了解我，那次的争论相当激烈。他不清楚我能做什么。其实我和其他人一样。只是我做事情的方式和别人有些不同。我可能需要别人的帮助，但我不怕找人帮忙。"

布拉斯科只有87磅，却能在杠铃推举锻炼中举起265磅的杠铃。他说这种锻炼很有必要，因为需要举起水枪和其他较重的设备。"我经常锻炼，每次都在健身房躺下锻炼。这对我的工作帮助很大，我们必须要强壮。因为我能举起很重的东西，所以我很擅长做需要移动重物的救援工作，比如搬动很重的金属碎片——像交通事故后那样的现场。"

95

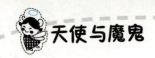
有火灾发生时，布拉斯科会穿上特制的防火服去救火。"我们只好拿出一套正常大小的防护服，然后把它裁剪到适合我的尺寸。当我第一次穿上这套衣服时，感觉棒极了。"

布拉斯科不去救火时，就在当地的百思买超市做兼职并努力学习，想成为一名帮助他人恢复健康的护士。但如果消防服务需要他，只要条件允许，他马上就去现场。"如果我在那个区域，我扔下东西就跑过去。"

布拉斯科希望他通过消防员基础考试后可以进入火场。"在那之前，我很高兴能在火场外帮忙并参加其他紧急情况的处理，但我知道我已经具备了相应的条件。"

　　"我下定决心做某件事情，我就会全力以赴。"这是一位身体残疾的青年的信念。正是依靠自己的一份执着、一种坚持，这位青年实现了自己的梦想。

　　打开梦想之门需要坚持，而坚持需要一颗执着的心。

　　哪怕这坚持的道路是多么漫长、崎岖，都不要轻易放弃。困难面前要告诉自己：坚持就是胜利！也许，再坚持一下，心中一个梦想便如雨后彩虹，挂在天空，绽放如天使般美丽的笑容。

执着天使篇

[之五]

Hold to Your Dream and Never Give Up

The lesson of the story is that instead of making dozen excuses why you can not realize your dreams, think about this story, just hold to your dream and never give up.

这个故事告诉我们，与其找借口解释梦想为什么不能实现，不如想想这个故事，坚持梦想，永不放弃。

The adolescent (青少年) girl from Tennessee is standing on the stage of a drama summer camp in upstate New York. It's a beautiful day. But the girl doesn't feel beautiful. She's not the leggy (腿修长), glamorous (富有魅力的) Hollywood type. In fact, she describes herself as dorky (傻).

Since she was six years old, Reese Witherspoon has wanted to be a country singer. And Dolly Parton is her idol (偶像). But this flat-chested (胸部扁平) wisp (一缕) of a girl is no Dolly Parton. Nevertheless, all of this summer she's been acting, dancing and singing–giving it her best.

Play to your strengths. If you're going to make it in this business, it's not going to be on sexy–that's not who you are. Better focus on what you're good at. Celebrate yourself.

Despite three years of lessons, at the end of camp her coaches tell her to forget about singing. They suggest she think about another career. If Reese did have talent, it was hiding under her skinny, mousy (灰褐色的) frame and her Coke-bottle glasses.

Still, she takes their words to heart. After all, why shouldn't she believe the professionals?

97

But back at home in Nashville, her mother—a funny, happy, upbeat (积极地) person—wouldn't let her mope (闷闷不乐). Her father, a physician, encouraged her to achieve in school. So she worked hard at everything and was accepted at Stanford University.

And at age 19, she got a part in a low-budget movie called *Freeway*. That led to a substantial (重大的) role in the movie *Pleasantville*. But her big break came with *Legally Blonde*.

Well, she decided, "If you can't sing and you aren't glamorous (富有魅力的), play to your strengths. If you're going to make it in this business, it's not going to be on sexy—that's not who you are. Better focus on what you've good at. Celebrate yourself." And then came the offer that took her back to her Nashville roots—playing the wife of tormented country star Johnny Cash, a singing role.

All of a sudden, the old fears were back. She was so nervous on the set, a reporter wrote, she "kept a sick bucket" nearby and admitted she "would go backstage (在后台) after a singing scene and shake". But she didn't give up on the movie or herself.

The humor and drive she learned at home overcame the self-doubt learned on that summer stage. She spent 6 months taking singing lessons again. She learned to play the Autoharp. And the hard work built up her confidence.

In March 2006, Reese Witherspoon walked up on another stage, the Kodak Theatre in Hollywood, and accepted the Oscar as Best Actress for her heartbreaking, heartwarming singing role as June Carter Cash in *Walk the Line*.

Finally, as you read these accounts of Reese Witherspoon, consider the obstacles she met. The lesson of the story is that instead of making dozen excuses why you can not realize your dreams, think about this story, just hold to your dream and never give up. (558 words)

(Extracted from "http://www.qnr.cn/waiyu/sy/sy/201110/706443.html")

坚持你的梦想，永不放弃！

一名少女由田纳西州来到纽约北部，她站在戏剧夏令营的舞台上，天气是那么好，她的心情却很糟糕。因为她不是那种身材颀长、丰腴美艳的好莱坞式美女，实际上她形容自己是"土里土气，还有点傻"。

从六岁开始，里斯·威瑟斯庞就梦想成为一名乡村歌手，多莉·帕顿是她心中的偶像。但她可一点都不像多莉·帕顿，她胸部扁平，身材纤细。然而，整个夏天她都竭尽全力地表演、跳舞和唱歌。

发挥长处。如果想在这一行发展，不要走自己不擅长的性感路线。更好地专注于自己的特长，为自己喝彩。

尽管她上了三年的声乐课程，夏令营结束时，老师们还是告诉她应该忘掉唱歌这件事儿，另谋出路。如果里斯确实有天分的话，那也是给她纤细的身材和厚如可乐瓶底儿的眼镜遮盖住了。

虽然心有不甘，可她还是听从了建议。毕竟，她有什么理由怀疑专业人士呢？

但回到位于纳什维尔的家里，她风趣、快乐、乐观的妈妈可不会让里斯感到丝毫的沮丧。她的爸爸是一名医生，他鼓励女儿在学业上有所成就。于是，她凡事努力，终于被斯坦福大学录取。

19岁那年，她出演了一部低成本电影《极速惊魂》。这为她后来在《欢乐谷》中争取到真正重要的角色奠定了基础。而她真正的破冰之作是影片《律政俏佳人》。

她暗下决心："既然自己没有歌唱天分，又不是光彩照人，那就发挥自己的长处。要想在这行做下去，就不要在性感上做文章了——自己不是

99

那种类型的。最好在自己擅长的方面下功夫，要展示自己。"这时，她接到片约，邀她出演约翰尼·卡什——一个饱受折磨的乡村歌手的妻子，这是个需要演员有唱功的角色，该片约又把她带回到纳什维尔的家乡。

突然，旧时所有的恐惧感又回来了，一名记者报道说，她在台上实在是太紧张了，甚至在一边"准备了呕吐时要用的痰盂"，她自己也承认"每唱完一幕回到后台，自己都在发抖"。但她没放弃那部电影，也没放弃自己。

她在家学到的幽默和动力克服了在夏季舞台上产生的自我怀疑。她用半年的时间再次学习声乐，还学会了演奏竖琴。不懈的努力让她重拾信心。

2006年3月，里斯·威瑟斯庞走上了另一个舞台——好莱坞的柯达剧院。凭借在影片《一往无前》里饰演的琼·卡特·卡什这一歌唱角色，她获得了奥斯卡最佳女演员奖，她在片中饰演的角色令人心碎，却温暖人心。

最后，当你读里斯·威瑟斯庞的故事时，想想她遇到的挫折。这个故事告诉我们，与其找借口解释梦想为什么不能实现，不如想想这个故事，坚持梦想，永不放弃。

巴斯德说过："告诉你使我达到目标的奥秘吧，我惟一的力量就是我的坚持精神。"只有执着地坚持自己的梦想，在你到暮年的时候，细细回想起来，才会觉得没有虚度曾经美好的年华，才会觉得自己的整个生命都充满价值。

不知道要走多少步才能达到目标，踏上第一千步的时候，仍然可能遭到失败。但成功就藏在拐角后面，除非拐了弯，我们永远不知道还有多远。再前进一步，如果没有看到桃花源，就再向前一步。事实上，每次进步一点点并不太难。相信自己，执着天使会指引我们走向成功！

嫉妒魔鬼

悲观魔鬼

胆怯魔鬼

自私魔鬼

虚荣魔鬼

魔鬼篇

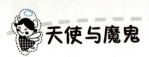

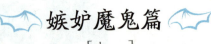

嫉妒魔鬼篇

[之一]

Rivals in Life

> Your rivals are not your opponents or those you grudge.
> Instead, they are your good friends!
>
> 对手既不是敌人也不是冤家，而是朋友！

Jaguar (美洲虎) is an endangered (濒危的) animal. It is said that there are less than 20 jaguars in the world currently, one of which is now living in the national zoo of Peru. In order to protect this jaguar, Peruvians singled out a pitch of land in the zoo for it, where there were herds of cattle, sheep and deer for the jaguar to eat. Anyone who had visited the zoo praised it to be the "Heaven of Tiger". However, strange enough, no one had ever seen the jaguar prey on the cattle and sheep. What we could see was its lying in its house eating and sleeping.

"It is normal for the jaguar to be lazy in this environment. Tiger is the king of forest but you simply put some small animals around it. That is why the jaguar shows no interest in going out. Why don't you put two wolves or at least a jackal around it?" a visitor proposed. Others all agreed with him and put five panthers (豹) into the jaguar's territory (领地). Since then, the jaguar did not go back to its house any more. It either stood on top of the hill roaring or went down from the hill strolling without sleeping all day long. It did not eat the meat provided by the zoo staff and had totally got back to its nature.

Actually, this principle does not only apply to animals, but also apply to human beings. Here is another story. There was a rich man who was selecting a husband for his only child among a multitude of pursuers. The man led all the pursuers to a river and pointed to the crocodiles, saying,

"Anyone who can swim across the river safe and sound will marry my daughter." Those pursuers looked at each other and no one dared to take the initiative. At that moment, a man plunged (投身入水) into the river bravely and swam at a staggering (令人震惊的) speed to the other side. All the people applauded for his courage with great sense of admiration. Nevertheless, the man, after landing on the bank, shouted angrily, "Who pushed me into the river just now?"

Maybe the man, after thinking of the whole process and the good consequence (结果) he is going to obtain, will feel obliged to the one who pushed him into the river. It is fairly common that disadvantages will turn into advantages and misfortunes into fortunes! But many of us cannot manage to realize the significance of our "rivals" to our success. Generally speaking, many people will see the one who "pushes him into the river" as an opponent. However, if you think in a deeper sense, you will realize that it is also a blessing and opportunity to have someone like that! It is the one who "pushes you into the river" that makes you feel the sense of crisis and stimulates your ambition and desire to strive! You will resolve to eliminate all difficulties and progress to another stage of your life!

In our world, one creature without any rivals is a lifeless creature. If a man lives without rivals, he is bound to be satisfied with the present and will not strive for the better. He would hold back before all difficulties and decline in inaction and laziness. Adverse environment tends to cultivate successful people. Therefore, your rivals are not your opponents or those you grudge (怨恨). Instead, they are your good friends! In our lives, we need some rivals to "push us into the river", leaving us striving ahead in all difficulties and competitions. In our work, we need some rivals to be picky about us and supervise our work with rigorous requirements and standards. Due to our rivals, we can bring out our potential to the best; due to our rivals, we will continuously promote our capabilities when competing with them! (639 words)

生活中需要对手

美洲虎是一种濒临灭绝的动物。据说，现在世界上尚存不足二十只，其中有一只生活在秘鲁的国家动物园。为了保护这只美洲虎，秘鲁人在动物园里单独圈出一块地，让它自由生活，圈地中有成群的牛、羊、鹿供它享用。参观过虎园的人都说这是"虎的天堂"。然而奇怪的是，没人看见这只老虎去捕捉牛羊，唯一见到的就是它躺在虎房里吃睡。

一位参观者建议道："在这种情况下美洲虎懒洋洋是很正常的。虎是林中之王，你们只是放一群小动物进去。这才是它没兴趣出来的原因。不放两只狼，至少也得放一只豺狗进去吧。"人们觉得他说得有理，就把五只美洲豹投进了虎园。结果，自从豹子进园后，美洲虎就再没回过虎房。它要么站在山顶长啸，要么从山上下来，在草地上游荡，不再长时间睡觉，不再吃管理员送来的肉，完全恢复了本性。

事实上，不仅是动物，人也如此。有这样一个故事，一位有钱人为独生女儿选丈夫，求婚者众多。这个富人将求婚的男子们带到一条河边，指着河中的鳄鱼说："如果有人能够安全地游到对岸，我就把女儿嫁给他。"这些男子你看我我看你，谁也不敢跳进河里。正在互相观望之际，突然有一个男子"扑通"一声跳了下去，然后以异乎寻常的速度游到对岸。大家对这个勇敢的男子充满钦佩和美慕，报以热烈的掌声。没想到这个男子上岸后，怒气冲冲地问："刚才是谁把我推下河去的？"

也许那位男子回过神来想一想整个过程和事后会得到的结果，他应该感谢那个把他推下去的人。不利变为有利，坏事变成好事，现实生活中比比皆是，但许多人往往认识不到造成这个结果的那个"对手"的作用。一般来讲，许多人都会把推他"下河"的人看作敌人。但只要仔细想一想，便会发现有一个那样的人，也是一种福分，一种机遇。因为这个推你"下河"的人，会让你产生危机感，会激发你旺盛的精神和斗志，会让你下定决心排除一切艰难险阻，实现人生新的超越！

在我们这个世界，一种没有对手的生物，是没有活力的生物。假如一个人没有了对手，他注定会变得安于现状，不思进取。他将知难而退，在怠惰和没落中消沉。逆境往往造就成功。所以，对手既不是敌人也不是冤家，而是朋友。人生中，我们需要一些对手推自己"下河"，让自己在阻力中前进，在竞争中发展。工作中，我们需要一些对手，对自己再三挑剔，严要求、高标准督促我们发现不足。有了对手，我们就会把自己的潜能发挥到极致；有了对手，我们就会在与对手的比拼中提高能力，不断进步。

每个人脑中都有一个头顶小角、身后丁字尾的恶魔；每个人胸中也都有嫉妒之心。关键是在生命中如何把嫉妒转化为动力，小说中那个笑傲江湖的"独孤求败"是悲哀的，没有对手永远是寂寞的，难怪"纳豆"和"小德"赛后脱水仍不忘夸赞对方、惺惺相惜，因为只有对手才能体现自己的价值，只有对手才能让我们找到动力。

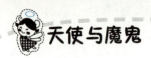

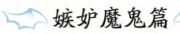 嫉妒魔鬼篇
[之二]

How to Deal with Bullies

> When your reaction to their hostility has inspired you to achieve further success, you've transformed the haters' negativity into fuel for your creative fires.
> 当你对待敌意的方式使你取得更大的成就的时候，嫉恨者的恶言恶语就会转变成熊熊烈火帮助你创造出更大的辉煌。

If you're someone who aspires to something beyond the ordinary, you must have figured out by now that there will always be those who are jealous or resentful (表示愤恨的) of your success.

It doesn't matter that you've worked long and hard to get where you are, nor that you've made great sacrifices in achieving your goals. The "haters" will always find a reason to criticize and even condemn (指责) you.

They're spiteful (居心不良的) people who begrudge (嫉妒) you the pride you have in yourself and the recognition you're receiving from others. They can't stand it that you're happy, fulfilled and achieving your goals.

These hateful individuals are unwilling to do the work that you've done; they rarely make the same kinds of sacrifices or put in the long, hard hours. They resent your success but are too lazy or spoiled to invest real time or energy in the pursuit of their own goals.

It's true that we aren't always going to succeed in our ventures, even if we put in the time and effort. Results are never guaranteed and life has a way of throwing curve balls at us.

I loved it when Tina Fey went up to collect her Golden Globe and held it high, saying, "This is for all the haters!" She's a good example of a

talented, hard—working and successful person who's received an inordinate amount of negative press. Ms. Fey may be besieged by haters but she refuses to let them get to her.

The thing you need to know about these haters is that the only reason they behave this way is that you have something they want but they aren't willing to work for it.

The haters are convinced that you've been lucky or that you've had some unfair advantage but the truth is that your success is born of your untiring efforts, and it's these efforts that have brought about your "luck".

The best way to deal with haters is what I call the "one—two punch". First, don't let them phase (干扰) you. Be happy about your success and proud of your accomplishments. Let in the approval and the recognition from affirming, supportive people and never doubt that you deserve all this. The haters are angry, jealous people. What they think or say is ultimately meaningless.

Next, the more the haters harass (侵扰) you, the more you should be motivated to succeed. They want to undermine (暗中破坏) you but your response should be to work that much harder in order to increase your level of success.

When your reaction to their hostility has inspired you to achieve further success, you've transformed the haters' negativity into fuel for your creative fires. Not only can they not hurt you but they've inadvertently spurred (鞭策) you on to even greater heights. (457 words)

如何应对
嫉妒你的人

如果你想与众不同，做出些非凡的成就，那你现在就一定要明白总有那么一些人会对你的成就心生嫉妒与怨恨。

无论你工作有多努力，或者你做出了多大的牺牲才获得了现在的成就，那些"恨你的人"总能找到理由来批评你，甚至诋毁你。

那些居心不良的人看不惯你对自己的成就的满足，也见不得你得到别人的认可。他们无法忍受你达成目标后的快乐、满足和成功。

这些嫉恨你的人不愿意去做你所做过的事，不愿意同你一样做出牺牲，也不愿意花时间去工作。他们只是嫉妒你的成功，却永远懒得去花时间和力气追求自己的目标。

诚然，有时候即使我们付出了时间和努力，也未必能成功。谁也不能保证生活会是一帆风顺的，有时，它也会打出曲线球。

我喜欢蒂娜·菲在金球奖领奖时说过的话，她把奖杯高高举起，说道："这是送给那些嫉恨我的人的！"蒂娜就是那种富有天赋、工作努力而且获得成功的好例子，同时，她也收到了无数负面抨击。蒂娜·菲虽然被困扰，但她不会受这些人的影响。

你只要记住：这些嫉恨你的人，他们会这样的惟一理由就是他们想得到你所得到的，却不愿意付出你所付出的。

讨厌你的人总觉得你只不过是运气好而已，或者你有某些他们觉得不公平的优势。但事实是，你是通过自己的不懈努力才做出了成绩，这些努力才是你的"好运"所在。

对付嫉恨你的人最好的就是下面这个办法，我称作"组合拳"。第一，别让他们影响到你。尽情地为自己取得的成功而感到高兴和自豪吧。

和那些欣赏你、赞美你、支持你的人在一起，千万不要怀疑自己是否应得这一切。讨厌你的人都是善妒易怒的人。他们所说所做，都不重要。

第二，那些人越是欺负你、骚扰你，你就越要积极地去获得成功。他们想要暗中使坏，而你的回应就是更加努力工作，取得更大的成就。

当你对待敌意的方式使你取得更大成就的时候，嫉恨者的恶言恶语就会转变成熊熊烈火帮助你创造出更大的辉煌。这些嫉妒你的人不但伤不了你，而且会鞭策你更上一层楼。

生活中总有你嫉妒的人和嫉妒你的人，面对你嫉妒的人你就化嫉妒为动力去赶超对方；而对待嫉妒你的人就坦然面对，用自己的成绩来回应那份嫉妒。当你对待敌意的方式使你取得更大成就的时候，嫉恨者的恶言恶语就会转变成熊熊烈火帮助你创造出更大的辉煌。

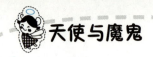

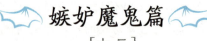 嫉妒魔鬼篇

[之三]

Difference

Chances exist in the daily details.

机遇就存在于生活的细节中。

John and Bobby joined a wholesale company together just after graduation from college the same year. Both worked very hard. After several years, however, the boss promoted (提升) Bobby to the position of manager while John remained an ordinary employee. John could not take it anymore, tendered his resignation (辞职书) to the boss and complained the boss did not know how to delegate (任命) and did not value hard working staff, but only promoted those who flattered (奉承) him.

The boss knew that John worked very hard for the years. He thought a moment and said, "Thank you for your criticism, but I have a request. I hope you will do one more thing for our company before you leave. Perhaps you will change your decision and take back your resignation."

John agreed. The boss asked him to go and find out anyone selling watermelon in the market. John went and returned soon. He said he had found out a man selling watermelon. The boss asked how much per kg? John shook his head and went back to the market to ask and returned to inform the boss $1.2 per kg.

Boss told John to wait a second, and he called Bobby to come to his office. He asked Bobby to go and find anyone selling watermelon in the market. Bobby went, returned and said, "Boss, only one person selling watermelon. $1.2 per kg, $10 for 10kg, he has inventory (存货) of 340

melons. On the table 58 melons, every melon weights about 2 kg, bought from the South two days ago, they are fresh and red, good quality."

John was very impressed and realized the difference between himself and Bobby. He decided not to resign but to learn from Bobby.

My dear friends, a more successful person is more observant (善于观察的), thinks more and explores in depth. Chances exist in the daily details. For the same matter, a more successful person sees more and farther so that he can find out an opportunity and catch it to realize his aim. If a person sees one year ahead, while another sees only tomorrow. The difference between a year and a day is 365 times, how could you win? (362 words)

(Extracted from "http://www.233.com/life/Daily/20110311/084227809.html")

差距

约翰和鲍比同年大学毕业后，进入同一家批发公司工作。他们二人工作都很努力。然而，几年后，老板提拔鲍比为经理，而约翰还是一名普通职员。约翰再也无法忍受，冲动之下写了一封辞职信，并抱怨老板不会用人，不重用那些敬业的员工，只提升那些奉承他的人。

老板知道这几年约翰工作确实很努力。他想了一会儿说："谢谢你对我的批评。但是我有一个要求，我希望在你离开之前再为公司做一件事情。或许到时你会改变决定，收回辞呈。"

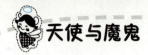
约翰同意了。老板让他去市场找一个卖西瓜的人。约翰去了并很快回来。他说他找到了一个卖西瓜的人。老板问他每公斤多少钱？约翰摇摇头，只好回到市场去问，然后又回来告诉老板每公斤1.2美元。

老板让约翰等一会儿，他把鲍比叫到办公室。他让鲍比去市场找到一个卖西瓜的人。鲍比去了，回来之后说："老板，只有一个卖西瓜的人，每公斤1.2美元，每10公斤卖10美元。这个人一共有340个西瓜，其中58个放在货架上，每个西瓜重约2公斤，都是两天前从南方运来的，新鲜，红瓤，质量好。"

约翰受到很大的触动，他意识到自己与鲍比之间的差距。他决定收回辞呈并向鲍比学习。

亲爱的朋友们，成功的人更善于观察，勤于思考和孜孜探求。机遇就存在于生活的细节中。同样的一件事，一个成功的人会看得更多更远，于是他能发现机遇并抓住它实现自己的目标。有人看到一年后的情景，而其他人只看到明天。一年与一天的差距是365倍，你怎么能赢呢？

当你面对一个优秀的人而心生嫉妒的时候，请及时将其转化为你前进的动力。比如看看我们嫉妒对方是因为对方有哪些长处，正是这些长处让对方引起我们的嫉妒，找到彼此的差距，经过努力，也许就会赶上对方，也许原有的嫉妒恶魔无意间就已经不见了。

嫉妒魔鬼篇
[之四]
Secretly Feel Good When Others Fail?

> The lower your self-esteem is, the more you'll experience schadenfreude.
>
> 你越自卑，就越会幸灾乐祸。

Do you rub your hands in glee (欢喜) if an acquaintance (认识的人) fails to land his dream job? Or chuckle when someone spills his coffee down his white shirt? If so, then it could be because you've got low self-esteem, according to researchers.

Enjoying someone else's misfortune is known as schadenfreude (幸灾乐祸) and scientists from Leiden University in the Netherlands say that the lower your self-esteem is, the more you'll experience it.

"If somebody enjoys the misfortune of others, then there's something in that misfortune that is good for the person," said study researcher Wilco W Van Dijk.

Van Dijk and his colleagues drew their conclusions after testing 70 undergraduates by asking them to read two interviews, reports LiveScience.

The first was about an ambitious student who was aiming to secure a dream job. The second was a chat with his supervisor (导师) who revealed that his academic success had been extremely patchy (部分尚好的) and that he wouldn't be offered the role.

The volunteers were then given various statements and asked to what degree they agreed with them.

113

天使与魔鬼

Their responses would measure their susceptibility (受影响的程度) to schadenfreude.

The statements included "I enjoy(ed) what happened to Marleen/Mark" and "I couldn't resist a little smile".

Self-esteem levels had been worked out in a separate test before this stage of the experiment and the results showed that those with a low opinion of themselves were happiest at learning of the student's misfortune.

To add even more veracity (真实性) to the study those with low self-esteem were tested again after they'd been given some short and intense positive thinking exercises – and their schadnfreude levels dropped.

Van Dijk told LiveScience, "I think when you have low self-esteem, you will do almost anything to feel better, and when you're confronted with the misfortune of others you'll feel schadenfreude."

"In this study, if we give people something to affirm theirselves, then what we found is they have less schadenfreude – they don't need the misfortune of others to feel better anymore." (327 words)

(Extracted from "http://www.12edu.cn/wyl/gjxw/201112/703447_2.shtml")

当别人失败时，
你会暗自发笑吗？

如果你认识的一个人没能获得梦想的工作，你是否高兴得摩拳擦掌？或者在某人把咖啡溅到白衬衫上时，你是否暗自发笑？研究人员说，如果是这样，那是因为你感到自卑。

因为别人的不幸而快乐就是幸灾乐祸。来自荷兰莱顿大学的科学家说，你越自卑，就越会幸灾乐祸。

114

研究人员维尔科·W·范·迪杰克说："如果某人因别人的不幸而感到高兴，那么别人遭受的不幸当中一定包含有利于这个人的地方。"

据"生活科学网站"报道，范·迪杰克和他的同事测试了70个大学生，让这些学生阅读了两份访谈而得出了这一结论。

第一份访谈是关于一个想获得梦想工作的雄心勃勃的学生。第二份访谈是该学生和导师间的谈话，谈话显示出他的学业成绩起伏很大，他将不能获得想要的工作。

研究人员向志愿者们提供了各种言论，并问他们在多大程度上同意这些言论。

从他们的反应可衡量出他们幸灾乐祸的程度。

这些言论包括"我对马琳/马克遭遇的事情感到高兴。"和"我忍不住感到一丝窃喜。"

在进行这一实验前，已经通过单独测试测出他们自尊心的强弱。结果显示，那些自卑的人在知道该学生的不幸后是最高兴的。

为了增强这一研究的真实性，研究人员在让那些自卑的人做了一些简短、强度大的正面思维训练后，又对他们做了一次测试，这次他们的幸灾乐祸程度下降了。

范·迪杰克告诉"生活科学网站"说："我认为当你自卑时，你几乎会做任何能让你感觉好起来的事情，因此在你知道他人遭遇不幸时，你会幸灾乐祸。"

"在这一研究中，如果我们向人们提供一些能让他们肯定自己的东西，我们就会发现他们就不会那么幸灾乐祸——他们不再需要用他人的不幸来让自己感觉好一些。"

人生中的有些事情我们处理起来往往缺乏自信、敬而远之，但是别人做起来我们却愿意幸灾乐祸，似乎别人做不成我们更高兴。正是嫉妒的恶魔在作祟，也正如本文所说"你越自卑，就越会幸灾乐祸。"幸灾乐祸没有意义，把幸灾乐祸的时间用来给自己充电吧，你会发现世界会豁然开朗。

115

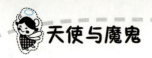

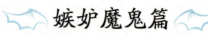 嫉妒魔鬼篇
[之五]

People Are Nicer to You, If They Think You Are Jealous of Them

> This fear of envy can encourage us to behave in ways that improve the social interactions of the group.
>
> 对嫉妒的恐惧可以鼓励我们改变自己的行为方式，以促进群体中的社交互动。

Successful people are nicer to those who are jealous of them, psychologists have found.

The fear that they may become the target of malicious envy makes people act more helpfully toward people who they think might be jealous of them.

Previous research found jealousy could be divided into benign (善意的) and malicious (恶意的) envy. Those with benign envy were motivated to improve themselves, to do better so that they could be more like the person they envied. However those with malicious envy wanted to bring the more successful person down.

The Dutch researchers then set out to question the effect on the target of the envy.

Niels van de Ven of Tilburg University said, "In anthropology, they say if you are envied, you might act more socially because you try to appease those envious people." He cited as an example the fisherman who shared his bigger catch around.

In lab experiments a group of people were made to feel like they would be maliciously envied by being told they would receive an award of five euros. Sometimes the prize was deserved and was based on the score they

were told they had earned on a quiz. But sometimes it was not based on their score at all.

The researchers thought that the deserved prize would lead to benign envy, while the undeserved prize would lead to malicious envy.

Then the volunteer was asked to give time-consuming advice to a potentially envious (嫉妒的) person.

People who had reason to think they would be the targets of malicious envy were more likely to take the time to give advice than targets of benign envy.

In another experiment, an experimenter dropped a number of erasers on the floor as the volunteer was leaving. Those who thought they would be maliciously envied were more likely to help him pick them up.

He said, "This sort of serves a useful group function. We all think better-off people should share with others but that's not something we are inclined to do when we are better-off." "This fear of envy can encourage us to behave in ways that improve the social interactions of the group."

The findings were published in *Psychological Science*, a journal of the Association for Psychological Science. (370 words)

人们对嫉妒自己的人更友善

心理学家发现，成功人士对那些嫉妒他们的人更友善。

因为害怕成为恶意嫉妒的对象，人们一般会更愿意帮助那些他们觉得可能会妒忌他们的人。

之前的研究发现，嫉妒可以分为善意嫉妒和恶意嫉妒。善意嫉妒者会积极提高自己、更好地表现自己以便能更接近自己嫉妒的对象。然而恶意嫉妒者则试图将比他成功的那个人拉下来。

一些荷兰研究者们开始讨论以上两类嫉妒者对嫉妒对象的影响。

蒂尔堡大学的尼尔斯·范·德·冯说："在人类学上，有观点认为如果你受到他人嫉妒的话，你可能会表现得更和善，因为你会试图安抚那些嫉妒你的人。"他举例说一个渔民如果钓到更大的鱼，他一般都会跟周围人分享。

在实验室实验中，一组人被告知将获得五欧元的奖励，以使他们感觉自己可能会遭到恶意嫉妒。这些奖励有的时候是根据他们所知道的测验成绩来发放的，是他们应得的；而有时候则完全不以测验成绩为依据。

研究人员认为，应得的奖励会引起善意嫉妒，而那些不应得的奖励则会招致恶意嫉妒。

接着研究人员让志愿者花时间给那些潜在的嫉妒者提一些建议。

相对于善意嫉妒的对象来说，那些觉得自己是恶意嫉妒对象的人们更愿意花费时间来提出建议。

在另外一个实验中，一位实验人员在志愿者离开时把一些橡皮掉到地上。那些认为自己遭到恶意嫉妒的人们更有可能会帮实验人员把橡皮捡起来。

该实验人员说："这种行为从某种程度上说是一种有用的群体功能。我们都认为境况更好的人应该跟其他人分享，但是当我们自己境况变好之后，我们并不愿意这样做。""而对嫉妒的恐惧可以鼓励我们改变自己的行为方式，以促进群体中的社交互动。"

以上研究成果发表在心理科学协会发行的《心理科学》杂志上。

每个人心中都有嫉妒的恶魔，但这也未必就是坏事。对嫉妒的恐惧可以鼓励我们改变自己的行为方式，人们对嫉妒自己的人会更友善，人们潜意识里不喜欢嫉妒的恶魔，自然希望打消别人的嫉妒动机，于是就会拉近彼此的距离，以促进群体中的社交互动。这就是嫉妒，亦善亦恶之物。

悲观魔鬼篇
[之一]

Gifts from the Fairy

Curse all the world's gifts for mockeries and gilded lies! I miscalled every one. How poor and cheap and mean I know those others now to be.

该死的礼物，都让我受人嘲笑和欺诈！每一样都叫错了。我现在才明白，其他礼物是多么低贱与卑劣。

In the morning of life came a good fairy with her basket, and said: "Here are gifts. Take one, leave the others. And be wary (谨慎), choose wisely! For only one of them is valuable."

The gifts were five: Fame, Love, Riches, Pleasure, Death. The youth, said eagerly, "There is no need to consider." and he chose Pleasure.

He went out into the world and sought out the pleasures that youth delights in. But each in its turn was short-lived and disappointing, vain and empty. In the end he said: "These years I have wasted. If I could but choose again, I would choose wisely."

The fairy appeared, and said: "Four of the gifts remain. Choose once more; and, oh, remember——time is flying, and only one of them is precious."

The man considered long, then chose Love; and did not mark the tears that rose in the fairy's eyes. After many, many years the man sat by a coffin, in an empty home. And he communed (谈心) with himself, saying, "Desolation (孤寂) after desolation has swept over me; but each hour of happiness the treacherous (奸诈的) trader, Love, sold me I have paid a

119

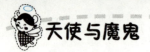

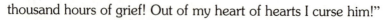

thousand hours of grief! Out of my heart of hearts I curse him!"

"Choose again," it was the fairy speaking, "The years have you wisdom—surely it must be so. Three gifts remain. Only one of them has any worth—remember it, and choose warily."

The man reflected long, then chose Fame; and the fairy, sighing, went her away. Years went by and she came again, "My name filled the world, and its praises were on every tongue, and it seemed well with me for a little while. How little a while it was! Then came envy; then detraction; then hate; then persecution (迫害). Then derision (嘲笑), which is the beginning of the end. And last of all came pity, which is the funeral of fame. Oh, the bitterness and misery of renown!"

"Choose yet again." it was the fairy's voice.

"Two gifts remain. And do not despair. In the beginning there was only one that was precious, and it is still here."

"Wealth—which is power! How blind I was!" said the man, "Now, at last, life will be worth the living. I will spend, squander (浪费), dazzle. These mockers and despisers will crawl in the dirt before me, and I will feed my hungry heart with their envy."

Three short years went by, and a day came when the man sat shivering in a mean garret; and he was gnawing a dry crust and mumbling (喃喃地说), "Curse all the world's gifts for mockeries and gilded lies! And miscalled every one. How poor and cheap and mean I know those others now to be. Bring it! I am weary. I would rest."

The fairy came, bringing again four of the gifts, but Death was wanting. She said, "I gave it to a mother's pet, a little child. It was ignorant, but trusted me, asking me to choose for it. You did not ask me to choose."

"Oh, miserable me! What is left for me ?"

"What not even you have deserved: the wanton insult of old age." (509 words)

(Extracted from "http://ts.hjenglish.com/page/159817")

仙女的礼物

　　在生命的起点，仙女降临到一个青年的身边，对他说："我这儿有几样礼物，你挑一个，其他的留下，一定要慎之又慎，因为最宝贵、最有价值的只有一件。"

　　一共有五份礼物：名声，爱情，财富，快乐，还有死亡。年轻人迫不及待地说："没有必要多想。"他选了快乐。

　　此后，他步入尘世，开始追寻属于年轻人的种种乐趣。但他所得到的快乐都是那么短暂，那么令人失望，那么虚无缥缈。最后，他叹到："我把那么多年的时光都浪费了，要是能再给一次机会，我一定能作出理智的选择。"

　　仙女出现了，她说："这里还有四份礼物。再选一次吧。噢，记住时间飞逝，而其中只有一件是珍贵的。"

　　他思考了很久，最终选择了爱情；他没有注意到仙女眼里泛起的泪光。许多许多年之后，这个人坐在一口棺材旁边，屋子里空荡荡的。他自言自语道："孤独一次又一次把我包围。都是因为爱情这个阴险狡诈的商人，他出售给我的每个甜蜜的小时，我现在都要用数千个小时的悲伤来偿还！我从心底里诅咒他！"

　　"你再选一次吧，"仙女又一次说话了，"这些年你已经变得有智慧了——也理当如此。这里还有三份礼物，其中只有一份是有价值的——切记，你好好挑吧。"

　　他想了很久，然后选择了名声。仙女叹了口气，径自离开了。岁月流转，仙女又回来了，站到他的身旁。"我的名字传遍世界，每个人都争相赞颂，有一阵子好像让我心满意足。可那是多么短暂的一阵子啊！随之而来的是妒忌；然后是诋毁；然后是憎恶；然后是迫害。之后是嘲讽，从一

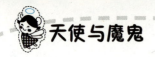

切开始步入完结。最后便是怜悯，这也是我的名声的葬礼。啊，名声原来是这般苦涩和痛苦！"

"不过你还可以重新挑一次。"仙女的声音再度响起。

"还剩下两份礼物。不要灰心丧气，从一开始就只有一份是宝贵的，而现在它还在那里啊。"

"财富——财富就是力量！我过去多盲目啊！"他说，"现在，终于，我的生命将要变得有意义。我要纵情欢度此生，我要挥霍我的人生。那些对我冷嘲热讽，轻蔑诋毁的人将要在我面前的泥土里挣扎，而我空乏的心也将因为他们的妒忌而得到满足。"

短短的三年又过去了。到了这么一天，这个人蜷缩在一个简陋的小阁楼里他一边啃着一块干面包皮，一边咕哝着："该死的礼物，都让我受人嘲笑和欺诈！每一样都叫错了。我现在才明白，其他礼物是多么低贱与卑劣。把它带来吧——那真正宝贵的礼物！我累了，我想休息了。"

仙女出现了，带着以前的那四件礼物，但惟独没有最后那一件——死亡。她说道："我把它给了一位母亲的宠儿：一个小孩子。他什么也不懂，但他相信我，让我来帮他挑选。而你并没有这么做。"

"哦，我多可悲啊！还有什么我可选的吗？"

"剩下的，你连得到的资格都没有，那就是年老体衰的折磨。"

悲观魔鬼让我们变得牢骚满腹、消极厌世。再好的东西透过悲观的眼睛也总能被冠以种种理由，难免遭到被抛弃的下场。悲观的人，客观和主观上都是不幸的，因为这样或那样得不到的幻影在折磨着他们脆弱的神经。

悲观魔鬼篇
[之二]

The Blue Day Book

> Then you'll spend the rest of your life looking over your shoulder, waiting for everything to go wrong all over again. This is crazy, because you're only young once and you're never old twice.
> 结果你得花掉下半辈子的时间回头看，等着一次又一次重蹈覆辙。这的确很蠢，因为你只能年轻一次，而且绝对不可能老两次。

Everybody has blue days.

These are miserable days when you feel lousy, grumpy (脾气暴躁的), lonely and utterly exhausted.

Days when you feel small and insignificant, when everything seems just out of reach.

You can't rise to the occasion.

Just getting started seems impossible.

On blue days you can become paranoid that everyone is out to get you.

This is not always such a bad thing.

You feel frustrated and anxious, which can induce a nail–biting frenzy (狂怒) that can escalate into a triple–chocolate–mud–cake–eating frenzy in a blink of an eye!

On blue days you feel like you're floating in an ocean of sadness.

You're about to burst into tears at any moment and you don't even know why.

Ultimately, you feel like you're wandering through life without purpose.

You're not sure how much longer you can hang on, and you feel like

123

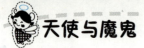

shouting, "Will someone please shout me!"

It doesn't take much to bring on a blue day.

You might just wake up not feeling or looking your best, find some new wrinkles, put on a little weight, or get a huge pimple (疙瘩) on your nose.

You could forget your date's name or have an embarrassing photograph published.

You might get dumped, divorced or fired, make a fool of yourself in public, be afflicted with a demeaning (有损人格的) nickname, or just have a plain old bad-hair day.

Maybe work is a pain in the butt.

You're under major pressure to fill someone else's shoes, your boss is picking on you, and everyone in the office is driving you crazy.

You might have a splitting headache, or a slipped dish, bad breath, a toothache, chronic gas, dry lips or a nasty ingrown toenail.

Whatever the reason, you're convinced that someone up there doesn't like you.

Oh what to do, what to dooo?

Well, if you're like most people, you'll hide behind a flimsy belief that everything will sort itself out.

Then you'll spend the rest of your life looking over your shoulder, waiting for everything to go wrong all over again.

All the while becoming crusty (易怒的) and cynical or a pathetic, sniveling victim.

Until you get so depressed that you lie down and beg the earth to swallow you up or, even worse, become addicted (沉迷于) to Billy Joel songs.

This is crazy, because you're only young once and you're never old twice. (392 words)

(Extracted from "http://ts.hjenglish.com/page/159817")

心情忧郁时别在悲伤的海里沉浮

谁都难免情绪低落。

在这样抑郁的时刻，你会变得心烦意乱，脾气暴躁，甚至会消极厌世。

当你感到渺小卑微的时候，当你孤独无力的时候。

你根本无法振作起来。

根本没有力气重新开始。

在忧郁的日子里，你可能变成偏执狂，觉得每个人都想要吃定你。

其实情况并不总是那么糟。

你感到灰心、焦虑，可能开始神经质地拼命咬指甲，然后不可救药地陷入一眨眼吃掉三大块巧克力蛋糕的疯狂！

在忧郁的日子里，你会觉得自己在悲伤的海里沉沉浮浮。

不论在什么时候，你总有种想哭的冲动，却不知道为了什么。

最后，你觉得自己犹如行尸走肉，失去生活目标。

你不知道自己还可以撑多久，然后你想大喊一声："谁来一枪把我打死吧！"

坏心情不需要什么特别的理由。

也许是因为早晨醒来，你感到身体稍有不适，或许是外表看起来不十分完美。一条新的皱纹，长胖了点儿，鼻子上鼓起的大疙瘩都会触动你脆弱的神经。

你可能忘记了约会对象的名字，或是有张可笑的照片被登出来。

你或许被人抛弃、离了婚，或是被开除，当众出丑，被刻薄的绰号弄得心乱如麻，或许只因为你得整天顶着一个其丑无比的发型。

125

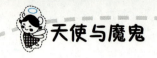
也许工作让你痛苦得如坐针毡。

你在强大的压力下顶替他人的位置，你的老板对你百般挑剔，办公室里的每一个人都让你发疯。

你可能会头疼欲裂，或重心不稳跌个正着，口臭、牙痛、不停放屁、口干舌燥，或是指甲长到肉里头了。

不管什么原因，你确定总是有人不喜欢你。

唉，该怎么办，到底该怎么办呢？

如果你像大多数人那样，不肯乐观起来，却又指望着烦恼自消自灭。

那么你的余生将会陷入后悔自责与重蹈覆辙的循环中。

与此同时，你会发现自己变成了易怒、消极、哀怨的可怜虫。

你会悲观到极点，恨不得化作一粒隔绝人世的尘土，乞求大地的收留。

若是沉溺于比利·乔的蓝调音乐中，你会更加难以自拔。

朋友，振作起来吧。因为你的生命中每一秒都转瞬即逝，请珍惜这宝贵的财富。

人有悲欢离合，月有阴晴圆缺，我们的心情自然不会静如止水。是否受制于消极情绪在悲观与乐观之间划定了界限。试想，一直悲观下去困窘就离我们而去了吗？倒不如让内心的坚强战胜哀怨的恶魔，即使周遭依旧暗淡，至少改善的希望会为我们的生活添彩。

悲观魔鬼篇
[之三]
Choose Optimism

The only thing more powerful than negativism is a positive affirmation, a word of optimism and hope.

唯一比否定态度更有力量的是一个积极的肯定，一句充满乐观与希望的话语。

If you expect something to turn out badly, it probably will. Pessimism is seldom disappointed. But the same principle also works in reverse (相反). If you expect good things to happen, they usually do! There seems to be a natural cause–and–effect relationship between optimism and success.

Optimism and pessimism are both powerful forces, and each of us must choose which we want to shape our outlook and our expectations. There is enough good and bad in everyone's life–ample sorrow and happiness, sufficient joy and pain–to find a rational basis for either optimism or pessimism. We can choose to laugh or cry, bless or curse. It's our decision: From which perspective do we want to view life? Will we look up in hope or down in despair?

An optimistic attitude is not a luxury; it's a necessity. The way you look at life will determine how you feel, how you perform, and how well you will get along with other people. Conversely, negative thoughts, attitudes and expectations feed on themselves; they become self–fulfilling prophecies (预言). Pessimism creates a dismal place where no one wants to live.

Years ago, I drove into a service station to get some gas. It was a beautiful day, and I was feeling great. As I walked into the station to pay

127

for the gas, the attendant said to me, "How do you feel?" That seemed like an odd question, but I felt fine and told him so. "You don't look well," he replied. This took me completely by surprise. A little less confidently, I told him that I had never felt better. Without hesitation, he continued to tell me how bad I looked and that my skin appeared yellow.

By the time I left the service station, I was feeling a little uneasy. About a block away, I pulled over to the side of the road to look at my face in the mirror. How did I feel? Was I jaundiced (患黄疸病的)? Was everything all right? By the time I got home, I was beginning to feel a little queasy. Did I have a bad liver? Had I picked up some rare disease?

The next time I went into that gas station, feeling fine again, I figured out what had happened. The place had recently been painted a bright, bilious (胆汁的) yellow, and the light reflecting off the walls made everyone inside look as though they had hepatitis (肝炎)! I wondered how many other folks had reacted the way I did. I had let one short conversation with a total stranger change my attitude for an entire day. He told me I looked sick, and before long, I was actually feeling sick. That single negative observation had a profound effect on the way I felt and acted.

The only thing more powerful than negativism is a positive affirmation (肯定), a word of optimism and hope. One of the things I am most thankful for is the fact that I have grown up in a nation with a grand tradition of optimism. When a whole culture adopts an upward look, incredible things can be accomplished. When the world is seen as a hopeful, positive place, people are empowered to attempt and to achieve. (532 words)

(Extracted from "http://www.djbkw.com/english/2009/0721/article_340.html")

选择乐观

　　如果你把事情往坏处想，结果往往不妙。悲观的人，通常会遭遇悲观事。同样，乐观的人和乐观的事总是联系在一起。心想好事，好事成！在乐观与成功之间似乎存在着自然而然的因果定律。

　　乐观与悲观对都会产生巨大的影响，两者徘徊在我们的期待与愿望之间，等待我们作出决择。每个人的生命中都有足够多的幸与不幸——数不清的哀伤和喜悦，欢欣与痛苦——给我们乐观或悲观的理由。我们可以选择哭或是笑，祝福或是诅咒。我们可以选择用什么样的眼光去看待生活——是昂首去寻找希望抑或垂头在绝望中逡巡。

　　乐观的态度不是一种奢侈品；它是我们生活的必需。你看待生活的方式将决定你的感受、你的表现，以及你与他人相处得怎样。反过来，悲观的想法、态度和预期也会自成因果；它们是能自我实现的预言。悲观会制造出无人愿去的黑暗处所。

　　几年前，我驱车去一个加油站加油。那天天气很好，我的心情也不错。当我走进加油站付油钱时，服务员问我："你感觉怎样？"问题问得有点古怪，但我感觉很好，于是便照实回答了他。他又说："你气色不好。"他的话让我非常吃惊。我告诉他我的感觉从未像现在这么好，但说此话时已不像原来那么底气十足。而他则毫无顾忌地继续大讲我的气色是如何差劲，还说我肤色发黄。

　　在离开加油站的时候，我觉得有点心神不宁。驶出一个街区之后，我把车泊在路旁，从镜中审视自己的脸。我怎么了？我得了黄疸病吗？是不是有什么异常？等我回到家里，我开始觉得有点恶心。我的肝脏出了毛病吗？是不是染上了什么怪病？

129

再次光顾那加油站的时候，我已恢复正常，感觉良好，而且明白了个中蹊跷。这个地方不久前把墙漆成了一种鲜亮的、胆汁般的黄色，这颜色使置身其中的每一个人都给映得像得了肝炎。不知道有多少人也曾有过和我相似的经历。和一个完全陌生的人的一次短短对话竟然改变了我整整一天的心情。他说我面有病容，很快我就真的觉得不舒服，仅仅是一个消极的看法就大大影响了我感觉和行为的方式。

积极的肯定，饱含着乐观与希望，是惟一能战胜消极心理的力量。最让我心存感激的事情之一就是我生长在一个有着光荣的乐观主义传统的国度。当一种文化从整体上采取了一种积极向上的态度，不可思议的事情也能变成现实。当人们把世界看作一个光明与希望之地，他们将被赋予努力进取和成就功业的力量。

悲观的恶魔逼使我们低下头，看到的全是些阴暗的角落。如果你足够勇敢的话，那么就冲破悲观那看似强大的阻力，向上看。把注意力集中在生活中光明的一面。当然，生命中总有伤痛，但是，当一切尘埃落定，你会发现生命中的美好远远比丑恶多得多。

悲观魔鬼篇
[之四]
The Last Leaf

> It is a sin to want to die.
>
> 想死是有罪过的。

At the top of a squatty, three-storey brick Sue and Johnsy had their studio. Mr. Pneumonia (肺炎) was not what you would call a chivalric (有武士气概的) old gentleman. A mite of a little woman with blood thinned by California zephyrs was hardly fair game for the red-fisted, short-breathed old duffer. But Johnsy he smote.

One morning the busy doctor invited Sue into the hallway with a shaggy (蓬松的), grey eyebrow. "She has one chance in – let us say, ten. And that chance is for her to want to live."

After the doctor had gone, Sue went into the workroom and cried a Japanese napkin to a pulp (纸浆). Then she swaggered (昂首阔步) into Johnsy's room with her drawing board.

Johnsy's eyes were open wide. She was looking out the window and counting – counting backward.

"Twelve," she said, and little later "eleven"; and then "ten", and "nine"; and then "eight" and "seven", almost together.

"Six," said Johnsy, in almost a whisper. "There goes another one. There are only five left now."

"Five what, dear? Tell your Sudie."

"Leaves. On the ivy vine. When the last one falls I must go, too."

131

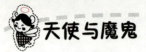

"Oh, I never heard of such nonsense," complained Sue, with magnificent scorn. "Well, the doctor told me this morning that your chances for getting well real soon were – let's see exactly what he said – he said the chances were ten to one! "

"Try to sleep," said Sue. "I must call Behrman up to be my model."

Old Behrman was a painter who lived on the ground floor beneath them. She told him of Johnsy's fancy.

When Sue awoke from an hour's sleep the next morning she found Johnsy with dull, wide-open eyes staring at the drawn green shade.

"Pull it up; I want to see," she ordered, in a whisper.

But, look! After the beating rain and fierce gusts of wind that had endured through the livelong (漫长的) night, there yet stood out against the brick wall one ivy leaf.

"It is the last one," said Johnsy. "I thought it would surely fall during the night. I heard the wind. It will fall today, and I shall die at the same time."

"I've been a bad girl, Sudie," said Johnsy. "Something has made that last leaf stay there to show me how wicked I was. It is a sin to want to die. "

The next day the doctor said to Sue, "She's out of danger."

And that afternoon Sue came to the bed where Johnsy lay, "I have something to tell you, white mouse," she said, "Mr. Behrman died of pneumonia today in the hospital. He was ill only two days. The janitor found him the morning of the first day in his room downstairs helpless with pain. They couldn't imagine where he had been on such a dreadful (可怕的) night. And then they found a lantern, still lighted, and a ladder that had been dragged from its place, and some scattered brushes, and a palette with green and yellow colors mixed on it, and ..." (507 words)

(Extracted and adapted from "http://novel.tingroom.com/shuangyu/42/1240.html")

最后一片叶子

在一处低矮的三层小砖楼的顶层，住着苏和琼西，她们的画室也设在这里。肺炎老先生可不懂得怜香惜玉，在加利福尼亚寒冷的冬天里弱不经风的年轻女子琼西成了他攻击的对象。琼西高烧不退，呼吸急促。

一天早晨，那个忙碌的医生扬了扬他那毛茸茸的灰白色眉毛，把苏叫到外边的走廊上。"我看，她的病只有十分之一的恢复希望，这一分希望就是她想要活下去的念头。"

医生走后，苏躲到画室伤心地大哭起来，泪水打湿了整张手帕。苏强忍着擦干了眼泪，故作镇定地背着自己的画夹，走进了琼西的房间。

琼西的眼睛睁得很大。她望着窗外，数着……倒过来数。

"12，"她数道，歇了一会又说"11"，然后是"10"和"9"，接着几乎同时数着"8"和"7"。

"6，"琼西几乎用耳语低声说道。"又掉了一片，只剩下五片了。"

"五片什么呀，亲爱的？告诉你的苏娣吧。"

"叶子。长春藤上的。等到最后一片叶子掉下来，我也就该去了。"

"哼，我从来没听过这种傻话，"苏十分不以为然地说，"瞧，医生今天早晨还告诉我，说你迅速痊愈的机会是，——让我一字不改地照他的话说吧——他说有九成把握。"

"你睡一会吧，"苏说道，"我得下楼把贝尔门叫上来，给我当模特儿。"

老贝尔门是住在她们这座楼房底层的一个画家。苏把琼西的胡思乱想告诉了他。

第二天早晨，苏只睡了一个小时的觉，醒来了，她看见琼西无神的眼睛睁得大大地注视拉下的绿窗帘。

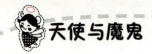
"把窗帘拉起来，我要看看。"她低声地命令道。

然而，看呀！经过了漫长一夜的风吹雨打，在砖墙上还挂着一片藤叶。

"这是最后一片叶子，"琼西说道，"我以为它昨晚一定会落掉的。我听见风声的。今天它一定会落掉，我也会死的。"

"我是一个坏女孩儿，苏娣，"琼西说，"天意让那片最后的藤叶留在那里，证明我是多么坏。想死是有罪过的。"

第二天，医生对苏说："她已经脱离危险。"

当天下午，苏来到琼西的床前，说："亲爱的，告诉你件事儿。"她接着说："贝尔门先生今天在医院因肺炎去世了。才病了两天。第一天早上，他躺在楼下浑身疼痛、动弹不得，是门房发现了他。大家都纳闷风雨交加的夜晚，他去哪呢。后来找到了个灯笼，还没灭呢，以及一把从别处挪过来的梯子，散落的画笔，调色板上有绿色混合着黄色的颜料，和……。"

悲观恶魔会带给我们什么呢？百害而无一利，甚至殃及关心和爱护我们的人。悲观的人用无助和脆弱换来了同情和关注。如果悲观的人不奋起与内心的恶魔反抗，最后只会枉费这一切的付出。悲观的人，可怜多些，还是可恨多些？

悲观魔鬼篇
[之五]
The Late Love Letter

> An optimist sees an opportunity in every calamity; a pessimist sees a calamity in every opportunity.
>
> 乐观的人在灾难中看到希望；悲观的人在希望中看到灾难。

I was always a little in awe of Great-aunt Stephina Roos. As I grew older I found, rather to my surprise, that I had become genuinely fond of my aloof old great-aunt. But to this day I do not know what strange impulse (冲动) made me take George to see her and to tell her, before I had confided (吐露秘密) in another living soul, of our engagement. To my astonishment, she was delighted.

She paused, as though she did not quite know how to begin.

"That was the happiest birthday of my life, for while we were resting between dances Richard took me outside into the cool, moonlit night, and there, under the stars, he told me he loved me and asked me to marry him. Of course I promised I would, for I was too happy to think of what my parents would say, or indeed of anything except Richard was not at our meeting place as he had arranged.

So when my father asked if I would drive with him to Driefontein I was delighted. Late that afternoon, Jantje, the little Hottentot herd boy, came up to me and handed me a letter, which he said the English baas had left for me. It was the only love letter I ever received."

The old lady came back from her dreams of that far-off romance.

135

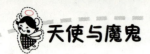

"Perhaps," she said, hesitating a little, "perhaps, my dear, you would care to read it?"

"I should love to, Aunt Stephia," I said gently.

She rose at once and tripped into the house as eagerly as a young girl. When she came back she handed me a letter, faded and yellow with age, the edges of the envelope worn and frayed (磨损) as though it had been much handled. But when I came to open it I found that the seal was unbroken.

"Open it, open it," said Great-aunt Stephia, and her voice was shaking.

I broke the seal and read.

It was not a love letter in the true sense of the word, but pages of the minutest (周详) directions of how "my sweetest Phina" was to go to "my true friend, Henry Wilson", who would give her money and make arrangements for her to follow her lover to Cape Town and from there to England, "where, my love, we can be married at once. If you do not come, and if I do not hear from you, then I shall know that you could never be happy so far from the people and the country which you love. If, however, you feel you can keep your promise to me, but are of too timid and modest a journey to England unaccompanied (单独), then write to me, and I will, by some means, return to fetch my bride."

I read no further.

"But Aunt Phina!" I gasped. "Why...why...?"

"But, Auntie, don't you even know what he wrote?"

The old lady looked down, troubled and shy like a child who has unwittingly (不经意地) done wrong.

"No, dear," she said, speaking very low. "You see, I never learned to read. (515 words)

(Extracted from "http://www.putclub.com/article.php?articleid=10887")

小的时候，我总对斯蒂菲娜姑妈心怀敬畏。后来，随着年龄的增长，另我惊讶的是，我打心眼里跟她亲近起来。在一种无以名状的冲动下，我带乔治去拜见她，把我们定婚的消息第一个告诉了她。真没想到，她竟然非常高兴。

她欲言又止，仿佛不知从何说起。

"那是我一生中最快乐的一个生日，因为理查德在舞会间歇把我带到屋外，在皎洁的月光下，当着点点繁星，他对我倾诉爱意，向我求婚。我毫不犹豫地答应了。当时被幸福冲昏了头脑，忘记了父母的约束，忘记了一切。脑海里只容得下他安排的见面地点。可是，他却一直没有现身。

所以，当父亲问我是否愿意和他一块开车去德里方丹时，我就高兴地答应了。那天傍晚，在我和父亲动身回家之前，霍但托特族的小牧童詹杰交给我一封信，他说是那位英国老爷留给我的。这可是我有生以来收到的惟一的情书。"

老太太从她那久远的爱之梦中醒过神来。"也许，"她带着犹豫的神情说，"也许，亲爱的，你想看看那封信吧？"

"我很想看，斯蒂菲娜老姑，"我轻声说。

她猛地站起身，奔进屋里，急切得像个小姑娘。她从屋里出来后，递给我一封信。由于时间久远，那信已经褪色发黄，信封边已经磨损，好像曾被摩挲过好多次。但在取信时，我发现封口还没有拆开。

"拆开，拆开吧，"斯蒂菲娜老姑声音颤抖地说。

我撕开封口，开始念信。

严格说来，它算不上是一封情书，实际上只是几页内容详尽的行动指

137

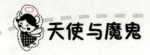

南。信里称"我最亲爱的菲娜"该怎么去找理查德的"知心朋友亨利·威尔逊",他会给她钱为她作好安排,使她能跟随她的情人到开普敦,随后转道英国。"亲爱的,这样我们就可以在英国结婚了。如果你不来,如果我听不到你的回信,我就会知道,如果你离开你挚爱的亲人和乡土,你是不会幸福的。但如果你能实践你对我的许诺而由于你生性持重胆怯不愿单身前往英国,就来信告诉我,那我就会设法回南非来迎接我的新娘。"

我没有再念下去。

"可是,菲娜老姑,"我气喘吁吁地说,"为什么……?为什么……"

"可是老姑,难道你一直不知道信里的事吗?"

老太太低头俯视着,像一个无心做错事的孩子一样怯生生的,不知说什么才好。

"不知道,亲爱的,"她用低沉的声调说,"你知道,我从来没有念过书啊!"

有的人宁可苟且活在悲观的阴影中,也不肯冲破胆怯的束缚而拥抱现实。孰不知无论这些人对悲观恶魔多么倔强地膜拜,多么虔诚地追随,它绝不会产生一丁点儿的怜悯之情,却义无反顾地将他们引向深渊。如果到了悬崖,还不肯挣扎着自救,结果只能是跌到痛苦的谷底。

胆怯魔鬼篇
[之一]
Beyond Fear

> We were all caring for our children, each in our own way.
>
> 我们都用自己的方式关心着我们的孩子。

When I was told last year that my 2-year-old son had an illness that threatened his life, I tried to strike a bargain with fate—I would do anything, I would trade my old life away, if only he would get better. We learned that our son would need months of treatment, maybe even a year, before we would know whether he would recover. My husband and I settled into a deadening routine; one night at the hospital, the next night at home to be with our daughter, then right back to the hospital. The days and nights were blurs (模糊的事物) of medical reports. Fear and despair engulfed (吞没) me.

After the first three weeks, we realized we were only at the start of a marathon. The friends who knew me best started telling me I should go back to work. It would be good for you to get a break, they said. I resisted. Good mothers, I thought, do not abandon (放弃) their sick children for work. Yet when my son's doctor told me he thought it would be fine, that he could email his assessments, I tore myself away.

I could not work a normal schedule—far from it. But as the months of my son's treatment dragged on, he was able to stay out of the hospital for longer periods. My husband and I still took turns at the outpatient clinic

139

or at the hospital. I was lucky that my family and my baby sitter could also relieve me so that my son was never alone.

There were still long stretches when I needed to drop everything to be with him. But to my surprise, I found that going to work when I could ease my sense of helplessness. I could be distracted; there were phone calls and deadlines and a rhythm to be swept into. I could be in control of something.

I felt guilty at first about the solace (安慰) I took from work. I often wondered what the other mothers thought of me—taking my work clothes to the hospital, showering in the parents' stall after a long night in which we'd heard the cries of all our children.

Eventually, I realized that getting away was good not only for me but for my son and daughter. When my son first became sick, the doctors told me I had to be strong for him. I could not show fear. Somehow I also had to convey confidence to my daughter, to help her endure what had befallen us.

Although I feared that working might be selfish, I could see that it actually seemed reassuring to my children, a sign that we could, for moments at least, return to our routines. Working was a pledge (保证) that life could go on. It was a statement of hope. I realized that I, like many others who care for sick people, needed somewhere else to go once in a while to draw breath and find meaning before returning to the work of nursing. For me, my job was that place. For others, it might be someplace else.

My son is recovering now, but I am still too close to his illness to understand fully what lessons I can learn, what meaning I can wrest (取得), from this experience. All I can say is that working when my child was so sick might look wrong from the outside, but on the inside, it helped keep me sane. I grew less intimidated (恐惧不安) by the other mothers. I allowed myself to see that I was no less dedicated (奉献的). We were all caring for our children, each in our own way. (607 words)

(Adapted from "http://www.chinaenglish.com.cn/html/c61/2009-12/36882.html")

超越恐惧

去年当我知道两岁的儿子患了一种危及生命的疾病时，我努力跟命运抗争，只要他能好起来，我什么都愿意做，甚至改变我以前的生活。我们了解到，我儿子需要几个月、甚至一年的治疗，才能知道是不是可以康复。我和我丈夫陷入了一种呆滞的生活中：前一晚在医院，第二天晚上在家陪女儿，然后又一晚待在医院。日日夜夜都是治疗报告。恐惧和绝望吞没了我。

前三周过后，我们意识到这只是一场马拉松的开始。了解我的朋友开始对我说，我应该继续工作。他们说，换换环境对我有好处。我拒绝了。我认为好母亲不会丢下生病的孩子去工作。然而儿子的医生也告诉我那样做会好一些，他可以用电子邮件向我传递治疗报告，我只好忍痛离开了。

我无法正常工作——远远不能。但儿子的治疗挨过了一个月又一个月，他可以出院在外待较长时间了。我和我丈夫仍然轮流去诊所或是医院。幸运的是，我的家人和保姆也能减轻我的负担，所以儿子一直有人陪着。

即使是这样，可仍有很长一段时间我得抛开一切事情陪在他身边。但让我吃惊的是，我发现只有在工作的时候才能减轻我的无助感。我可以分散注意力，因为有那么多电话要处理，那么多紧急的和常规的工作要去做。我还能够管理某些事情。

刚开始我觉得从工作中获得安慰有一种内疚感。我常常想到别的母亲会怎么看我——我把上班穿的衣服带到医院，熬了长长的一晚听够孩子们的哭闹后在家长单间里冲澡。

最后，我意识到离开不仅对我而且对我儿子女儿都有好处。儿子刚开始生病的时候，医生就对我说，为了他我得坚强起来。我不能把恐惧显露出来。我还得设法把信心传递给女儿，帮她承受降临在我们身上的事情。

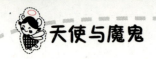

尽管我也担心我去工作可能自私了一些，但我知道实际上这消除了孩子们的疑虑，这表示我们至少有时可以回到正常的生活中去。工作意味着生活能继续。工作也说明有希望。我认识到，我也像其他患者的家人一样，需要不时地去其他地方歇一歇，找到生活的意义，然后再回去照料病人。对我而言，工作就是这样一个换换气的地方。对别人来说，可能是其他地方。

我儿子现在正在恢复，但我仍很担心他的病情，以致于不完全知道从这次经历中我能吸取什么教训、得出什么结论。我能说的只是孩子生病我还工作，在外人看来这似乎是不对的。但实际上，这样做帮助我保持理智。我不再因为其他母亲的行动而感到不安。我自己也看到我跟其他母亲一样乐于献身。我们都用自己的方式关心着我们的孩子。

每个人因为不同的原因都会心生恐惧，这胆怯恶魔甚至可能陪伴我们终生，然而"人有畏惧多自警"，真正意识到恐惧了，我们反而会更勇敢和坚强，去面对问题和解决问题。发现恐惧之始，亦是超越恐惧之时。

胆怯魔鬼篇
[之二]
Fear of Change

> Looking back now, I can see it was fear that was holding me back.
>
> 现在回过头来看，当时是恐惧使我止步不前。

Looking back now, I can see it was fear that was holding me back. Not fear of dying. Fear of trying. I was afraid to succeed. I was afraid to be different. I was afraid to walk away from a fight. Why? Because for most of my life, I didn't know any other way to be.

I'm from Niagara Falls. A beautiful place, you think. And you'd be right, if you were talking about the Canadian side, the part that tourists flock (聚集) to. But I'm from the other side of the Falls, the New York side, which is a big ghetto (贫民区).

Since I was the oldest of us four kids, I ended up being the man of the house. It fell to me to protect my siblings, and even my mom, and I got into a lot of fights, too many to count.

I left my mom's house by the time I was 16, dropped out of high school, and got my own place at 17. I had a son at 19. That was kind of a wake-up call to get my act together. I got my GED. Then my associate's degree, doing work-study to pay for tuition (学费).

The degree helped me land a job as a computer technician. Not the most exciting work, but it was legit. That didn't mean I stopped fighting, though.

I felt a pull to leave home, but I was afraid. I had the scars, the tattoos (纹身) and the bald head. I fit the stereotype (固定模式) of a guy from the

143

slum, the kind they showed on TV. The guy looked as he's going to flip(击打) at any moment.

I prayed for direction and out of the blue. One night, a friend I hadn't heard from in a couple years called. She was living in Charlotte, North Carolina. "Why don't you come down here?" she said. It was pretty obvious what I needed to do.

I left home, left the Falls. I should have failed when I got to Charlotte. I only knew one person in the city. I didn't have a job lined up, and after 9/11, a lot of opportunities dried up.

The one job I found was at a call center run by OnStar. The call center was staffed 24-7, and hundreds of people worked there, who I never would've met otherwise. We'd talk during breaks. Every one of them was interesting. Everybody had a dream. I learned customer service. And I learned not to take things personally.

But the biggest thing that I learned came out of an argument I had in the cafeteria one day with a coworker. My coworker, a manager, used to be a teacher in Canada, so I liked to call him The Professor. We got into it talking about African American males. I said guys like me just didn't get the same opportunities others did. The Professor contended(主张) that people of any race felt stuck in their circumstances because they were afraid to change. He gave me a book, a paperback. *Feel the Fear and Do It Anyway* by Susan Jeffers. "Promise me you'll read it from front to back," he said.

So I did, cover to cover. It really opened my eyes. The book totally changed me.

My imagination was on fire. I would open a bookstore, I decided. I wanted to open other people's eyes, to feed their minds. I talked to my coworkers about my dream in February 2004. I had six books to my name. By the end of March, I had 3,000.

I saved up money, got two small-business loans with a partner's help, and leased a retail space.

RealEyes opened its door that December. I sell new and used books. I put in 50, 60 hours a week. It's hard work keeping a dream alive, but you know what? I'm not afraid to try. (639 words)

(Adapted from "http://source.yeeyan.org/view/276430_cca/Courage%20to%20Change")

对于改变的恐惧

现在回过头来看，当时是恐惧使我止步不前。我不是惧怕死亡，而是惧怕改变、惧怕成功。我害怕改变自己，害怕面临一场打斗而转身离去。为什么会这样呢？因为我的大部分生活就是在打架中度过的，除此之外我不知道还能怎样生活。

我来自于尼亚加拉瀑布区。你会这样想这是个美丽的地方啊。你说得不错，如果你说的是加拿大那边的话，那里是旅游者们蜂拥而至的地方。但我是来自于瀑布区的另一边，纽约市的这边，一个大贫民窟。

因为我是四个孩子中最大的，自然就成了当家的男人。我要保护我的兄弟姐妹，甚至保护我的母亲。我因此经常和人打架，次数多得都数不清了。

我十六岁时离开了家，从高中辍学，十七岁时有了自己的栖身之所。十九岁时有了一个儿子。是儿子唤醒了我的责任感，使我觉得应该做些该做的事情了。我先是拿到了普通教育学历证书，然后通过半工半读付学费，取得了副学士学位。

我的学业帮助我找到了一份电脑技术员的工作。这份工作虽然平淡无趣，但毕竟是正式合法的。不过这并不意味着我就此停止和别人打架斗殴了。

我有一种想要离家出走的冲动，但又害怕。我身上有伤疤、纹身，还是光头。我就是电视里所表现的那种典型的贫民区青年的形象，那种随时都可能惹事的人。

我祈求上帝给我指引方向，带我走出困境。一天晚上，一位几年未见面的朋友给我打来电话。她住在北卡罗来纳州夏洛特市。"为什么不到这里来呢？"她说。很显然这就是我应该做的。

我离开了家，离开了瀑布区。到夏洛特后我本不会顺利的。在这座城市里我只认识一个人。也没有现成的工作等着我，9·11事件后工作机会更是贫乏。

我只找到了一份在OnStar公司呼叫中心的工作。呼叫中心每周7天每天24小时都要有人值班，有几百号人在那里工作。要是不去那里工作，我可能永远也遇不到他们。休息时我们就在一起聊天，他们每个人都很有趣。人人都有梦想。我学会了如何为顾客服务。还学会了不以个人情感去处理问题。

但我学到的最主要的一件事来自于和一个同事在餐厅里的一场争论。我的这位同事是个经理，过去曾在加拿大的一所学校当教师，所以我喜欢称呼他教授。我们谈论起美国非洲裔男性的话题。我说像我这样的人根本得不到和其他人同等的机会。教授不同意我的说法，他说任何种族的人都会感到无法摆脱他们的处境，因为他们害怕改变。他给了我一本书，一本平装书。是苏珊·杰弗斯写的《感受并克服恐惧》。"答应我把它从头读到尾。"他对我说。

我真的好好读了，每一页都认真读了。这本书的确打开了我的眼界。这本书彻底地改变了我。

我的想象力被激发了。我决定要开一家书店。我也要打开其他人的眼界，去充实他们的心灵。2004年的2月份我告诉了同事们我的梦想。那时我只有6本书。到三月底我已经有了3000本。

我用积攒的钱以及在一个合作伙伴的帮助下借的两笔小生意贷款租赁了一个店铺。

那年的十二月我的"真实眼睛"书店开张了。我卖新书也卖旧书。每周我都要工作五六十个小时。要实现并维持一个梦想就要付出艰辛的努力，但是你知道吗？我不再惧怕为一个新的目标而奋斗了。

人更喜欢安于现状、随波逐流，对于年龄、容貌、环境、财富等，人们往往对改变充满了恐惧，这胆怯恶魔一直都在。现在回过头来看，是恐惧使我们止步不前。若想不再一成不变，首先要打破的就是对改变的恐惧。

胆怯魔鬼篇
[之三]
Know What's Causing the Shyness

> Shyness is the effect of feeling insecure.
>
> 害羞的根源是不安全感。

What are the situations that trigger (引发) your shyness? Despite what you may think, you're not shy all the time. For example, when you're with your best friend, you're probably very open and comfortable being yourself. Realize that shyness is the effect of feeling insecure (不安全的). If you can identify (指出) what you're feeling insecure about, you can then take action on it.

Improve on your areas of insecurity

After identifying your areas of insecurity, the next step is to take action on them. For example, perhaps you are shy when it comes to presentations at work. If that's the case, then work on improving your presentation skills! Invest your 10,000 hours of hard work—it's been said that 10,000 hours is the average time experts spend to be the best at their skills.

Identify your strengths

Many of us tend to focus on what we're not good at, rather than recognize what we are good at. As a result, we feel awkward (笨拙的) around others, because we feel there's nothing to impressive about ourselves. It's time to stop selling yourself short ages and start focusing on your strengths. What are you good at? What are your past achievements (成就)? What are things you've done that you are really proud of? Spend some time to recognize them.

147

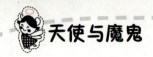

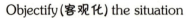

Objectify(客观化) the situation

Many people worry too much about what others think about them. But the funny thing is, it's just in your mind. Most people are actually too busy thinking about themselves to pay attention to what you're doing or not doing.

Have a role model

Can you think of someone (whether a friend or a famous person) you know who is very confident, assured and outgoing? Use the person as your role model. Whenever you feel shy, ask yourself what that person will do/say in this situation. Then, do that. Soon, it becomes second nature to you to behave in that manner.

Observe how others interact(互相影响)

A great way to overcome shyness is to observe how others around you act. Reduce the time you spend worrying about how others perceive you and look outward at how others conduct themselves socially. What do they say? How do they act? What can you learn from them? (368 words)

(Extracted from "http://258en.com/en/2011_1017/7547.html")

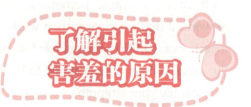

了解引起
害羞的原因

在什么情况下你会害羞？尽管你知道，你肯定不是所有时候都害羞。比如，当你和最好的朋友在一起、或者一个人的时候，你肯定会感觉很放松。要知道，害羞的根源是不安全感。只有你知道了令自己感到不安全的是什么，你才能有针对性地采取行动。

改善自己的不安全感

当你知道自己在哪些方面感到不安全后，下一步就是采取行动了。比如，也许你在汇报自己的工作时感到害羞，那么去花10000个小时改善你的演讲技能吧！据说那些在某个领域最出色的专家们在训练他们的技能上所花费的平均时间是10000个小时。

认清自己的优势

很多人都把注意力放在自己的劣势上，而往往忽略了自己的优势。这样一来，我们就会觉得自己一无是处。是时候开始关注自己的长处啦！花时间想想：我擅长做什么？我有过哪些成就？我做过哪些令自己引以为荣的事情？

客观看待问题

很多人都过于在乎别人怎么看自己了。但有趣的是，这只是你自己的想法。实际上大部分人都忙于考虑自己的事情而根本没注意你做了什么或者没做什么。

找个榜样

你能想到一个充满自信、开朗外向的朋友或名人吗？把他当作你的榜样吧。一旦你害羞了，问问自己他在这种情况下会怎么做、会怎么说，然后向他学习。很快，这种行为方式也就会成你的第二天性。

观察别人

一种克服害羞的好方法是观察别人怎么做。不要去想别人怎么看你，把时间花在观察他们怎么行动上。他们怎么说？怎么做？你能从他们身上学到什么？

社交场合，即使外向一些的人也要在熟悉环境的基础上进一步表现自己，不安全感是害羞的根源。因为胆怯恶魔作祟，我们不能正常表现自己，以至于害羞、封闭。认清自己能做什么、擅于做什么，也许能更放得开，你最拿手的东西自然收放自如。

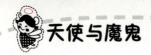

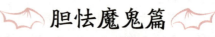 胆怯魔鬼篇

[之四]

About Death

> And most important, have the courage to follow your heart and intuition.
>
> 最重要的是，要勇于听从你内心的直觉。

When I was 17, I read a quote that went something like, "If you live each day as if it was your last, someday you'll most certainly be right." It made an impression on me, and since then, for the past 33 years, I have looked in the mirror every morning and asked myself, "If today were the last day of my life, would I want to do what I am about to do today?" And whenever the answer has been "No" for too many days in a row, I know I need to change something.

Remembering that I'll be dead soon is the most important tool I've ever encountered (遇到) to help me make the big choices in life. Because almost everything—all external (外在的) expectations, all pride, all fear of embarrassment or failure—these things just fall away in the face of death, leaving only what is truly important. Remembering that you are going to die is the best way I know to avoid the trap of thinking you have something to lose. You are already naked. There is no reason not to follow your heart.

About a year ago I was diagnosed (诊断) with cancer. I had a scan at 7:30 in the morning, and it clearly showed a tumor (肿瘤) on my pancreas (胰腺). I didn't even know what a pancreas was. The doctors told me this was almost certainly a type of cancer that is incurable, and that I should expect to live no longer than three to six months. My doctor advised me to

150

go home and get my affairs in order, which is doctor's code for preparing to die. It means to try to tell your kids everything you thought you'd have the next 10 years to tell them in just a few months. It means to make sure everything is buttoned up so that it will be as easy as possible for your family. It means to say your goodbyes.

I lived with that diagnosis all day. Later that evening I had a biopsy (活组织检查), where they stuck an endoscope (内窥镜) down my throat, through my stomach and into my intestines, put a needle into my pancreas and got a few cells from the tumor. I was sedated, but my wife, who was there, told me that when they viewed the cells under a microscope the doctors started crying because it turned out to be a very rare form of pancreatic cancer that is curable with surgery. I had the surgery and I'm fine now.

This was the closest I've been to facing death, and I hope it's the closest I get for a few more decades. Having lived through it, I can now say this to you with a bit more certainty than when death was a useful but purely intellectual concept:

No one wants to die. Even people who want to go to heaven don't want to die to get there. And yet death is the destination we all share. No one has ever escaped it. And that is as it should be, because Death is very likely the single best invention of Life. It is Life's change agent. It clears out the old to make way for the new. Right now the new is you, but someday not too long from now, you will gradually become the old and be cleared away. Sorry to be so dramatic, but it is quite true.

Your time is limited, so don't waste it living someone else's life. Don't be trapped by dogma—which is living with the results of other people's thinking. Don't let the noises of others' opinions drown out your own inner voice. And most important, have the courage to follow your heart and intuition (直觉). They somehow already know what you truly want to become. Everything else is secondary. (636 words)

关于死亡

17岁的时候，我读到了一句格言，好像是："如果你把每一天都当作生命中最后一天去生活的话，肯定有一天你会是正确的。"这句话给我留下了深刻的印象。从那以后，在过去的33年中我每天早晨都会对着镜子问自己："如果今天是我生命中的最后一天，我会去做原本今天打算做的那些事吗？"每当答案连续多日都是"不会"的时候，我知道我该做些改变了。

提醒自己我即将死去，是帮我做出人生中许多重大抉择的最重要的工具。因为几乎所有的一切——所有他人的期望、荣耀、对于困窘或失败的恐惧——这些在死亡面前都会消失殆尽，留下的是真正重要的东西。提醒自己将要死去，我认为是避免患得患失的最好办法。你本来就一无所有，没有理由不顺心而为。

大约一年前，我被诊断出得了癌症。我在早晨7点半做了扫描，扫描结果清楚地显示我的胰腺上长了一个肿瘤。我当时甚至都不知道胰腺是什么东西。医生告诉我，这基本上是一种无法治愈的癌症，我剩下的时间不会超过3-6个月。医生劝我回家，安排后事，这是医生让病人等死的婉言。这意味着你要尽量把本来想在未来10年内对孩子们说的话在几个月里说完；意味着你要把一切安排妥当，让你的家人尽可能地轻松一点；意味着你要说"再见"了。

诊断结果让我想了一整天。那天晚上晚些时候，我做了活组织切片检查。医生将一个内窥镜从我的喉咙伸进，通过我的胃，进入我的肠子，然后用一根针刺进我的胰腺，在肿瘤上提取了一些细胞。我当时注射了镇定剂，但在场的妻子后来告诉我，医生在显微镜下观察这些细胞的时候，忽然叫了起来，因为我患的竟然是一种非常罕见的、可以用手术治愈的胰腺癌。我做了手术，现在痊愈了。

那是我与死神擦肩而过的一次，我希望这也是以后几十年最接近死神的一次。以前死亡对于我只是一个有用但抽象的概念，有了这次经历后，我现在可以更加确信地对你们说：

没有人愿意死，即使人们想上天堂，也不会为了去那里而死去。但是死亡是我们每个人共同的归宿，无人幸免。也应该如此，因为死亡很可能是生命惟一最好的发明。它是生命变化更替的推动力。它破旧立新。你们现在是新人，但是不久的将来，你们会慢慢变老，然后被清除掉。我很抱歉这很戏剧性，但事实就是这样。

你们的时间很有限，所以不要浪费时间在重复别人的生活。不要受教条的束缚，因为那就意味着你依据别人的思想在生活。不要让他人喋喋不休的意见淹没掉你自己内心的声音。最重要的是，要勇于听从你内心的直觉。可以说，内心的直觉早已知道你想要成为什么样的人，而其他一切都是次要的。

本文是2005年乔布斯在斯坦福大学演讲的节选，是其中的第三个故事"关于死亡"。每个人在面临死亡的时候都会有恐惧，但是所有的人都要知道我们迟早会面临这一天。克服心中对死亡的恐惧，同时把每一天都当成最后一天，心中拥有紧迫感，跟随我们的直觉，追求自己的梦想。

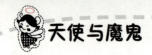

胆怯魔鬼篇
[之五]
Quarter-Life Crisis

"Setting the clock back on adulthood and starting again" brings with it a sense of freedom.

"把成年的时钟指针往回拨并重新开始"将带来自由的感觉。

They may still be in the prime (精华) of their lives, but for many young adults, their 20s and 30s are now a time of panic and self-doubt as they suffer a "quarter-life crisis".

Faced with too many choices, they are experiencing the traditional symptoms of a mid-life crisis earlier, research suggests.

Today's young adults often struggle with the multitude (多数) of options available, driving them to feel anxiety, depression and a sense of being trapped or "locked into" a marriage or a job that doesn't feel right.

And the phenomenon appears to be more common than in the past, according to Greenwich University researcher Oliver Robinson.

Dr. Robinson, who interviewed 50 people aged between 25 and 35 about their difficulties coping, said, "You are now more footloose to make changes in early adulthood than I think you once were."

"There is greater fluidity (多变性) in the job world, greater fluidity in marriage or alternatives to marriage. This fluidity has meant a major life changes are more acceptable."

"In the past, if a major life changes were to occur, it would happen in mid-life."

"Pressure to meet parents' demands can add to the sense of crisis among today's young adults," he said.

"It is about people feeling a frenetic need to get a job, make money and be successful quickly," said the researcher.

"It links to the demanding nature of people in their 20s and 30s who want it all. They are not happy with a mediocre (平凡的), dull, conventional life."

While a major re-evaluation of life choices can be unsettling, it seems to be worth it in the end, the British Psychological Society's annual conference heard.

Dr. Robinson said, "setting the clock back on adulthood and starting again" brings with it a sense of freedom.

And those who have suffered–or are in the midst of–a "quarter–life crisis" will be glad to know that it cuts their odds of suffering a "proper" mid–life crisis later on.

Dr. Robinson said, "You'd be much less likely to suffer another crisis because the lifestyle that you have post crisis is intrinsically (本质地) healthier than what you had before." (362 words)

(Extracted from "http://www.en8848.com.cn/read/bi/mentalhealth/140922.html")

青年危机

很多二三十岁的年轻人也许还处于人生的黄金时期，但因为遭遇"青年危机"，他们正在恐慌和自我怀疑中挣扎。

研究表明，由于面临太多选择，他们正提早经历中年危机的一些传统症状。

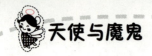

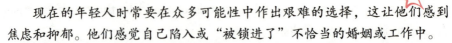

现在的年轻人时常要在众多可能性中作出艰难的选择，这让他们感到焦虑和抑郁。他们感觉自己陷入或"被锁进了"不恰当的婚姻或工作中。

格林威治大学的研究人员奥利佛·罗宾森认为，和过去相比较，现在"青年危机"的现象更普遍了。

在调查了50位年龄在25岁到35岁之间的人应对危机的情况后，罗宾森博士说："如今在刚步入成年期时作出改变比以前要随意。"

他说："职场和婚姻的变动性更大，替代婚姻的生活方式也更多。这一变动性意味着重大的人生改变更易于接受。"

"在过去，重大的人生改变一般在中年时期发生。"

他说，为了实现父母期望而产生的压力增加了现在年轻人的危机感。

研究人员说："这种危机感体现在急迫地要找到工作、赚钱以及迅速成功。"

"二三十岁年轻人的危机感和他们想要得到一切的苛求心态有关。他们无法满足于平庸、枯燥的传统生活。"

不过，这份在英国心理学会年会上提交的研究报告称，尽管重新衡量人生选择的过程会使人焦虑，但最后看来，似乎还是值得的。

罗宾森博士说，"把成年的时钟指针往回拨并重新开始"将带来自由的感觉。

有一点会让那些曾经经受过或正在经受"青年危机"的人感到安慰，那就是"青年危机"会降低他们以后遭受真正的中年危机的可能性。

罗宾森博士说："你遭受另一场危机的可能性会大大降低，因为青年危机后的生活方式从本质上来讲比你先前的生活方式要健康。"

面对"青年危机"也不必过分紧张，在年龄面前任何人心中的胆怯都会更加强烈。能否可以像成年人那样妥善地解决这些不确定的因素呢？本文中"把成年的时钟指针往回拨并重新开始"只是一种安慰与暗示，然而我们要体会年龄带来的成熟恩惠，把每个年龄段该做的事情做好，相信就不会"少壮不努力，老大徒伤悲"了。

自私魔鬼篇
[之一]
The Selfish Giant

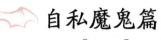

When there was golden fruit in every other garden, there was no fruit in the giant's garden. It was always winter there with the north wind, and snow, and ice, and driving rain.

当别的花园结满金色的果子时，巨人的花园里却一个果子也没有。那儿永远是冬季，有凛冽的北风、寒冷的冰雪和飘泼的大雨。

Every afternoon, as the children were coming back from school, they used to go and play in the giant's garden. It was a beautiful large garden. Beautiful flowers grew in the grass. There were twelve fruit trees. In the spring the fruit trees were covered with red and white flowers, and later in the year they bore rich fruit. The birds sang in the trees so sweetly that sometimes the children stopped their games and listened to them. "How happy we are here!" they cried to each other.

One day the giant came back. He had been away for seven years. When he arrived, he saw the children playing in his garden. "What are you doing here?" he cried in a very loud voice. The children ran away. "My own garden is my own garden," said the giant, "I will allow no one to play in it but myself." So he built a high wall round it and put up a notice: Keep out. He was a very selfish giant.

So the children had nowhere (无处) to play.

The spring came, and there were flowers and little birds all over the country. But in the garden of the Selfish Giant it was till winter that the birds did not like to sing in it because there were no children, and the trees

157

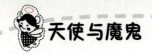

forgot to bear flowers. When there was golden fruit in every other garden, there was no fruit in the giant's garden. It was always winter there with the north wind, and snow, and ice, and driving rain (倾盆大雨).

The giant was lying in bed one morning when he heard some beautiful music. It was a little bird singing outside his window. It was so long since he had heard the song of a bird that it seemed to him the most beautiful music in the world. Then the north wind and the rain stopped.

"I believe that spring has come at last!" said the giant. He jumped out of bed and looked out.

What did he see? He saw a most wonderful sight. The children had come in through a hole in the wall and were sitting in the branches (分支) of the trees. There was a little child in every tree that he could see. The trees were so glad to have the children back that they had covered themselves with flowers; the birds were flying about and singing with joy, and flowers were looking up through the green grass.

"How selfish I have been!" said the giant. "It's your garden now, little children," said the giant, and he pulled down the wall. When the people were going along the road to the town, they found the giant playing with the children in the most beautiful garden they had ever seen. (460words)

(Extracted from "http://www.sunjua.com/page/main/news_show.php?id=107979&p=1")

自私的巨人

　　每天下午，孩子们放学回来后都会到巨人的花园玩耍。那个花园又大又漂亮。草丛中盛开着美丽的花朵。花园里栽了12棵果树，春天的时候，树上会开满红色、白色的花儿；到了秋季，树上硕果累累。鸟儿在树上清脆地歌唱，连孩子们也被吸引，驻足倾听。孩子们不禁欢呼："我们多么快乐啊！"

一天巨人回到了花园，他已经离开七年了，当他看到有孩子在他的花园玩儿，大吼道："你们在这儿干什么呢？"孩子们闻声跑开了。巨人又说："我的花园只属于我一个人，除了我，谁也别想在这儿玩。"于是，他在花园周围筑起了高墙，还贴了告示：禁止入内。他可真是个自私的家伙。

孩子们因此没有玩的地方了。

春天来了，全国到处开满鲜花，鸟儿到处飞。但是在自私的巨人的花园里却仍是一派残冬的景象——因为园内没有孩子的踪迹，鸟儿也就不愿在这儿歌唱，连树都忘了开花。当别的花园结满金色的果子时，巨人的花园里却一个果子也没有。那儿永远是冬季，有凛冽的北风、寒冷的冰雪和飘泼的大雨。

一天早上巨人躺在床上，忽然听到一种优美的音乐。这是一只小鸟在窗外唱歌。他已经很久没听到鸟儿的歌声了，所以他以为这是世上最美的音乐。接着，北风息了，暴雨停了。

"我相信春天到底来了！"巨人说着跳下床朝外面看去。

他到底看到了什么呢？他看到了十分美妙的景致。孩子们从围墙上的一个窟窿钻进来，然后爬到树枝上，坐在那儿唱歌。他目光所及的每棵树上都有孩子灵巧的身影。树木因孩子们的到来而兴奋不已，连树上的花儿都开了；鸟儿欢快地飞来飞去，它们的叫声又变得清脆嘹亮；草丛中的花儿又扬起了笑脸，加入这快乐的派对。

"我以前太自私！"巨人如此感叹，他又说："孩子们，这里从今以后就是你们的花园了。"于是，他推倒了围墙，进城路过此地的人们看到了巨人和孩子们在花园里一起嬉戏，这个花园是他们眼中最美丽的。

自私恶魔集贪婪、嫉妒、报复、吝啬和虚荣于一体。自私的人不愿与他人分享快乐，而将自己"囚禁"；自私的人抢夺不属于自己的幸福，损毁他人的利益，他的世界没有以此而繁荣。恰恰相反，自私者被局限在荒凉的小岛，那个岛屿的名字是"自我"。

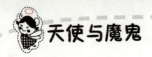

自私魔鬼篇

[之二]

Selfish Outlook Vanished When We Turn 33

The age at which we are most selfish is our teenage years, researchers found—with people saying that just growing up made them more likely to consider others.

研究发现：我们最自私的时候是在青少年时期，人们都说是成长让他们更多的考虑到了别人。

It's no longer 'me, me, me': Selfish outlook vanished (消失) when we turn 33. When you're fed up with self-obsessed (自恋的) twenty-somethings, try to remember that they'll be 33 one day. For that's the age when they lose the 'all about me' attitude, research suggests.

By then, youthful selfishness subsides and people begin to consider others' feelings more often, researchers say.

When we reach 33, we are also more likely to make an effort with parents and grandparents and take a positive attitude towards ending feuds with family or friends.

The older we get, the more selfless we are in almost all areas of life with the exception of volunteering in the community, the report suggests.

Most people agree that having children is the turning point in changing our attitudes towards other people. This is when we apparently find ourselves worrying more about others and doing things for them, such as checking how they are getting home, offering to help with childcare and doing airport runs.

And we are more likely to keep an eye out for neighbors, as well as give up seats to elderly people on public transport. We will probably also be more involved in the community and willing to donate money to good causes.

Those under 33 are most likely to admit to being very selfish—with 40 per cent saying that they put themselves first in all circumstances. However, 40 per cent of this age group regularly volunteer (自愿) for charity (慈善机构) or their community—higher than any other age group.

The age at which we are most selfish is our teenage years, researchers found, with people saying that just growing up made them more likely to consider others.

Others cited meeting their partners or buying a house as the point at which they started being more compassionate (富有同情心的) and putting others first.

Researchers at Make-A-Wish Foundation UK, a charity which grants wishes to youngsters fighting a life-threatening illness, came to their conclusion after studying the attitudes of 2,000 adults aged from 20 to 60. Spokesman Emma Cronin said, "It's never too early to put other people before yourself." (349words)

(Extracted from "http://www.hjenglish.com/new/p231923")

33岁后人不再自私？

161

自私的心态会在我们33岁的时候变得最轻微。于是，我们不会心里只想着：我要这样，我要那样。也许你会对那些20来岁年轻人自恋自私的做法忍无可忍，可是记住，他们到了33岁这个年龄会有改变的。有研究表明，33岁这个年龄会扭转以自我中心的态度。

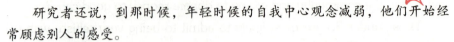

研究者还说，到那时候，年轻时候的自我中心观念减弱，他们开始经常顾虑别人的感受。

到了33岁，我们往往会更注重改善与父母或祖父母的关系。更加乐于消除与亲戚朋友间的隔阂。

研究表明，随着年龄的增大，几乎在生活中的各个领域，我们会越来越无私，当然在社区做志愿者服务的人除外（他们一直都无私）。

很多人都认为有了小孩是我们改变对待他人方式的一个转折点。这也是我们能很明显就能够察觉到自己更加地关心别人，帮助别人的时候，比如关心他们如何回家，帮忙照顾他人的孩子，接送机等。

同时，我们更有可能照顾到邻里了，如在公交车上为老人们让座。我们更有可能更加深入社区活动，愿意做好事，捐赠。

33岁以下的人多数都会承认他们非常自私——40%的人说，在任何环境他们都会把自己放到第一位。然而，这个岁数以下的40%的人经常为慈善组织或他们的社区做志愿服务，这个比例比其他的年龄群都要高。

研究者发现：我们最自私的年纪是青少年时期，人们都说是成长让他们更多地考虑到了别人。

其他人认为经历过谈恋爱，买房子这些事情后，人们开始变得富有同情心，变得"先人后己"地考虑问题了。

英国愿望成真基金会致力于帮助身患绝症的年轻人实现梦想。该基金会对2000名20至60岁的成年人进行调查后，得到同样结论。其发言人克罗宁女士认为："先人后己，越早越好。"

曾经有人为"人之初性本善"还是"人之初性本恶"而争论不休。实际上，随着年龄的增长我们渐渐懂得富有同情心、为别人考虑会带给我们自己更多的快乐的道理。自私的人，驱走内心的恶魔吧！当无私的行为让生命的价值得到最大程度的发挥时，你会感受到自己内心的美好，而且整个世界也更加令人愉悦。

自私魔鬼篇
[之三]
Beautiful Heart

I have some rough edges, which I cherish, because they remind me of the love we share.

我十分珍惜这些疤痕，因为它们能使我想起我们共同拥有的爱心。

One day a young man was standing in the middle of the town proclaiming (宣告) that he had the most beautiful heart in the whole valley. A large crowd gathered and they all admired his heart for it was perfect. There was not a mark or a flaw in it. Yes, they all agreed it truly was the most beautiful heart they had ever seen. The young man was very proud and boasted more loudly about his beautiful heart.

Suddenly, an old man appeared at the front of the crowd and said, "Why your heart is not nearly as beautiful as mine." The crowd and the young man looked at the old man's heart. It was beating strongly, but full of scars. It had places where pieces had been removed and other pieces put in, but they didn't fit quite right and there were several jagged (锯齿状的) edges. In fact, in some places there were deep gouges where whole pieces were missing.

The people stared—how can he say his heart was more beautiful, they thought? The young man looked at the old man's heart and saw its state and laughed. "You must be joking," he said, "Comparing your heart with mine, mine is perfect and yours is a mess of scars and tears."

163

"Yes," said the old man, "Yours is perfect looking but I would never trade with you. You see, every scar represents a person to whom I have given my love–I tear out a piece of my heart and give it to them, and often they give me a piece of their hearts which fits into the empty place in my heart, but because the pieces aren't exact, I have some rough edges, which I cherish (真爱), because they remind me of the love we share. Sometimes I have given pieces of my heart away, and the other person hasn't returned a piece of his heart to me. These are the empty gouges–giving love is taking a chance. Although these gouges are painful, they stay open, reminding me of the love I have for these people too, and I hope someday they may return and fill the space in my heart. So now do you see what true beauty is? "

The young man stood silently with tears running down his cheeks. He walked up to the old man, reached into his perfect young and beautiful heart, and ripped (撕) a piece out. He offered it to the old man with trembling (发抖的) hands.

The old man took his offering, placed it in his heart and then took a piece from his old scarred heart and placed it in the wound in the young man's heart. It fit, but not perfectly, as there were some jagged edges. The young man looked at his heart, not perfect anymore but more beautiful than ever, since love from the old man's heart flowed into his. They embraced and walked away side by side. (490 words)

(Extracted from "http://www.rrting.com/English/shyy/150924")

美丽的心

一天，年轻人站在城中向大家炫耀他有一颗山谷中最美的心。很多人围观，赞叹他的心的确完美，既没有疤痕也没有瑕疵。人们心服口服地表示，他们没见过比这更美的心了。年轻人听后，越发骄傲起来，对自己的心如何美丽大加吹嘘。

突然，人群中一位老人现身了，说道："我怎么觉得你的心不及我的心好看呢？"大家和年轻人都朝老人家看去，那颗心强有力地跳动着，但却布满了伤痕。有的地方破碎了，又填上了补丁，补丁的边缘粗糙不平。甚至有的地方缺失了大块，留下深深的豁口。

人们都惊呆了——他们想不通老人家为什么声称自己拥有比年轻人更美丽的心。年轻人不屑于老人家那颗心破碎的外表，嘲笑着说："你开什么玩笑，把你的心跟我的心比比看，你的分明就是破烂不堪的心嘛！"

"是的，"老人说，"你的心从表面来看很完美，但我绝不会跟你交换。你看，每个伤疤都代表我为别人献出的一份爱——我掏出一块心给他们，他们常常会掏出自己的一块回赠给我，但由于这两块不完全一样，伤口的边缘就留下了疤痕，不过我十分珍惜这些疤痕，因为它们能使我想起我们共同拥有的爱心。有时我送出了心，其他人并没有回赠给我，因此就出现了这些深孔——献出爱只是创造机会。尽管这些伤口疼痛，并且整日敞开着，却能使我想起我给予他们的爱。我希望有一天，他们能够回来填补上我心里的空间。你们现在明白什么是真正的美丽了吧？"

年轻人默默无语地站着，泪水顺着脸颊流下。他走到这位老人身边，

165

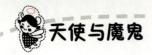

把手伸进自己完美而年轻美丽的心里，撕下一块儿来。他用颤抖的双手把它献给这位老人。

老人接过馈赠，把它放进自己的心里。然后他从自己疤痕累累的心里掏出一块，放在年轻人心里的那个伤口上。正好放进去，但不是特别吻合，因为有一些疤痕。年轻人看着自己的心，它不再完美但比以前更美丽了，因为老人心中的爱也流淌到了他的心里。他们互相拥抱，然后肩并肩离开了。

自私的人出发点是为自己尽可能多地谋得好处，哪怕牺牲他人的利益。往往自私的魔鬼损人却不利己，因为自私的人的内心是孤零零的。无私看似给予别人的甚至多于自己的收获，然而爱由此也流向更广阔的地方，无私的人互相拥抱，肩并肩地前进，社会也会因他们而更加和谐。

自私魔鬼篇
[之四]

Three Snake-leaves

> As selfishness and complaint cloud the mind, so love with its joy clears and sharpens the vision.
>
> 自私和抱怨使心灵阴暗，愉悦的爱则使视野明朗开阔。

The king had a daughter who was very beautiful, but there was also something very strange about her. She had made a vow to take no man for her lord and husband unless he promised to let himself be buried alive with her if she died before him. This strange vow had hitherto deterred (阻止) all suitors, but a young man was so entranced by her beauty that he was heedless of everything, and asked her father for her hand. Then the king consented and the marriage was celebrated with great magnificence.

They lived happily and contentedly for a time, and then it happened that the young queen fell seriously ill and no doctor could help her. She died. When the day came for the queen's dead body to be laid to rest in the royal vault, the young king was taken down into it with her.

As he sat there staring in front of him, he saw a snake crawl out of one corner of the vault and approach the coffin. He drew his sword and exclaimed (大叫), "You shan't touch her so long as I am alive!" And he hacked the snake into three pieces. A few moments later a second snake came crawling out of the corner, but when it saw the other one lying dead and dismembered (分割) it turned back, and presently approached again

167

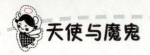

carrying three green leaves in its mouth. The dead snake stirred and came to life again, and both snakes crawled quickly away leaving the leaves behind them.

The unfortunate young king picked up the leaves and laid one of them on the dead woman's mouth and the other two on her eyes. Scarcely had he done so when she was revived (复活). The young king took the three snake-leaves with him, gave them to a servant and said, "Keep them carefully for me, and carry them on you wherever you go."

Since being brought back to life the young queen had undergone a change: it was as if all her love for husband had been drained out of her heart. On a voyage she killed the young king with the ship's captain. But the faithful servant restored the young king to life with the three snake-leaves.

Then they both rowed a small boat day and night with might and main, they got home to the old king before the others. When he heard of his daughter's wickedness (邪恶) he said, "I can't believe that she did so evil a thing, but the truth will soon come to light." Soon after the big ship came sailing in, and the prince's godless wife appeared before her father with a sorrowful air. She cried, "I have come home in great grief: during the voyage my husband suddenly fell sick and died. "

The old king told the two men to come out and said to his daughter, "There can be no mercy for you: he was ready to die with you, and he gave you your life back again, but you murdered him in his sleep and you shall have your just reward." Then she and her accomplice (同谋者) were put on board a ship full of holes and sent out to sea, where they soon perished in the waves. (550 words)

(Extracted and adapted from "http://www.enfang.com/english/c13/2009-12/15335.htm")

蛇的三片叶子

国王有个漂亮的女儿，只是她的性情比较古怪。因为她曾经发誓只有同意在她死后被一起活埋的人才能娶她。这个非比寻常的誓约几乎吓跑了所有的追求者，只有一个年轻人似乎对公主的美貌着了魔，竟然不顾一切地向国王求婚。国应允了，并且为公主和年轻人举行了盛大的婚礼。

他们一起幸福快乐地过了一些日子。突然，年轻的王后患了重病，医生们都认为不可救药了。王后死了。在年轻的王后遗体装进王家墓穴的那一天，那年轻的国王也被一同带进墓穴。

正当他一动不动向前看着的时候，突然见到墓穴的一角爬出一条蛇，直向棺材爬去。于是，他拔出宝剑说："只要我还活着，你就别想碰她。"他把这条蛇砍成三段。不一会儿，又一条蛇爬了过来，看见这条蛇死了并被分了尸，就立刻退回去了。随后那条蛇叼着三张绿叶又出现了。死了的蛇，又复活了，动弹了。接着，两条蛇很快地爬走了。可绿叶还留在那儿。

于是他拣起三片叶子，一片放在妻子的嘴上，另两片放在眼睛上。刚放好她就复活了。年轻的国王带回来了三片蛇的叶子，把它们交给了仆人说："好好保存着，要随身携带。"

自从王后复活后，变化很大，好像对丈夫的爱，一下子全都消失了似的。在一次航海中，她和船长一起杀死了年轻的国王。可是，那个忠实的仆人用带在身边蛇的三片绿叶让年轻国王复活了。

他俩夜以继日地拼命划着一艘小船，终于他们赶在其他人之前回到老国王那里。老国王得知了女儿的恶行后说："我简直不敢相信她竟如此恶毒，真相自会揭晓。"不久，大船归航了，那无法无天的妻子装作悲伤的

169

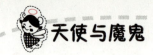

样子来见老国王，她哭着说："回来的路上，我十分难过，因为我的丈夫病死了。"

老国王叫出了两个人，对女儿说："我绝对不会饶恕你的。你的丈夫甘心情愿为你而死，而且他对你有救命之恩。可你却在他熟睡时杀害了他。等待你的将是正义的惩罚。"随后，她和船长被一起装到了一艘凿满了窟窿的船上。船被推到了海里，很快他们被海浪吞噬了。

自私的恶魔把人们内心的自我欲望膨胀起来，自我欲望的阴影弥盖了他人的言语、行为、思绪。然而，世间万物都有着千丝万缕的联系，一旦主观刻意将必然的联系生硬改变为单一方向，那么回报的也许是暂时的蝇头小利，但必然会用更大的损失作为自私的惩罚。

自私魔鬼篇
[之五]
Missed Happiness

> A man is called selfish, not pursuing his own good, but neglecting his neighbor's.
>
> 追求自身的利益，不是自私；忽视他人的利益，才是自私。

A young man was getting ready to graduate from college. For many months he had admired a beautiful sports car in a dealer's showroom, and knowing his father could well afford it, he told him that was all he wanted.

As Graduation Day approached (临近), the young man awaited signs that his father had purchased the car. Finally, on the morning of his graduation, his father called him into his private study. His father told him how proud he was to have such a fine son, and told him how much he loved him. He handed his son a beautiful wrapped gift box. Curious, but somewhat disappointed, the young man opened the box and found a lovely, leather-bound (用皮革包边的) Bible, with the young man's name embossed in gold.

Angrily, he raised his voice to his father and said, "With all your money you give me a Bible?" He then stormed out of the house, leaving the Bible.

Many years passed and the young man was very successful in business. He had a beautiful home and a wonderful family, but realizing his father was very old, he thought perhaps he should go to see him. He had not seen him since that graduation day. Before he could make the arrangements, he received a telegram (电报) telling him his father had passed away, and

171

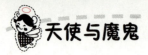

willed (遗赠) all of his possessions to his son. He needed to come home immediately and take care of things.

When he arrived at his father's house, sudden sadness and regret filled his heart. He began to search through his father's important papers and saw the still new Bible, just as he had left it years ago.

With tears, he opened the Bible and began to turn the pages. As he was reading, a car key dropped from the back of the Bible. It had a tag with the dealer's name, the same dealer who had the sports car he had desired. On the tag was the date of his graduation, and the words… "PAID IN FULL".

How many times do we miss blessings (祝福) because they are not packaged as we expected? I trust you enjoyed this. Do not spoil what you have by desiring what you have not; but remember that what you now have was once among the things you only hoped for. Sometimes we don't realize the good fortune we have or we could have because we expect "the packaging" to be different. What may appear as bad fortune may in fact be the door that is just waiting to be opened. (422 words)

(Extracted from "http://www.putclub.com/article.php?articleid=10867")

错过的幸福

一位年轻人即将大学毕业的时候，相中了一辆摆在展厅中的帅气的跑车。对于他富有的父亲来说买下它是件很轻松的事情。为了实现这数月以来的愿望，他向父亲提出了这个要求。

随着毕业典礼的临近，儿子越发盼望听到关于那辆跑车的好消息。毕业典礼当天上午，父亲把他叫进来自己的书房。告诉他能拥有这样优秀的儿子他十分自豪也非常非常爱他。说完，父亲递给儿子一个漂亮的礼盒。儿子好奇地打开礼物的包装，但是令他失望的是父亲送他的原来是一部精致的用真皮裹边的《圣经》，上面用烫金印着年轻人的名字！

　　失望迅速变成了愤怒，年轻人大喊："你有万贯家财，就送我这个？"他冲了出去，把《圣经》扔在身后。

　　时间荏苒，年轻人事业蒸蒸日上，他还拥有了幸福美满的家庭。想起父亲渐渐年老体衰，他动了回去看望一下的念头。毕竟那一别至今，从未与父亲谋面。令他措手不及的是，一封电报通知了他父亲已经辞世的噩耗，父亲把遗产全部留给了他。他必须回去打理好父亲的身后事。

　　一进到父亲的家门，悲伤和后悔顿时涌上他的心头。在查找父亲重要文件的过程中，他又看到了数年前被他抛弃的那本依旧崭新的《圣经》。

　　他打开了这本《圣经》，泪水模糊了双眼。当他翻看的时候，一把车钥匙从封底掉了下来。钥匙上系着当年那家跑车店的标签，上面赫然写着"全部车款已付清"，落款日期正是他毕业那天。

　　想想有多少幸福因为包装不尽人意而被我们错失？你一定也曾有过这样的遗憾。千万别让你的幻想破坏了你所拥有的现实。要知道从前的向往很可能已经变成了现实的一部分，有时候仅仅是形式上的差异便让我们对已经或将要得到的幸福视而不见。往往暂时的失望却是等待开启的通往幸福之门。

　　有的人在自私的行为之后，会经历稍纵即逝的沾沾自喜，有的人就不那么幸运了，遗憾甚至是悔恨则要相伴很久，甚至想不起来起初的自私究竟为了什么。自私恶魔通常都是带着人们钻进了功利的死胡同，倘若能及时自拔，扔掉有损他人的私欲，前面的路则由窄变宽了。

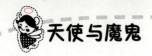

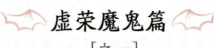
Having the Cookie

Happiness does not have anything to do with the cookie; it has to do with being alive.

　　幸福与小甜饼并非息息相关，而是与生命的存在有关。

One of my patients, a successful businessman, told me that before his cancer he would become depressed unless things went a certain way. Happiness was "having the cookie". If you had the cookie, things were good. If you didn't have the cookie, life wasn't worth a damn. Unfortunately, the cookie kept changing. Some of the time it was money, sometimes power, sometimes sex. At other times, it was the new car, the biggest contract (合约) and the most prestigious (有名望的) address. A year and a half after his diagnosis of prostate (前列腺) cancer he sat, shaking his head ruefully (悲伤地). "It's like I stopped learning how to live after I was a kid. When I give my son a cookie, he is happy. If I take the cookie away or it breaks, he is unhappy. But he is two and a half and I am forty-three. It's taken me this long to understand that the cookie will never make me happy for long. The minute you have the cookie it starts to crumble or you start to worry about it crumbling (破碎) or about someone trying to take it away from you. You know, you have to give up a lot of things to take care of the cookie, to keep it from crumbling and be sure that no one takes it away from you. You may not even get a chance to eat it because you are so busy just trying not to lose it. Having the cookie is not what life is about."

My patient laughs and says cancer has changed him. For the first time he is happy. No matter if his business is doing well or not, no matter if he wins or loses at golf. "Two years ago, cancer asked me, 'Okay, what's important? What is really important?' Well, life is important. Life. Life, any way you can have it, life with the cookie, life without the cookie. Happiness does not have anything to do with the cookie; it has to do with being alive. Before, who made the time?" He pauses thoughtfully, "Damn, I guess life is the cookie." (349 words)

(Extracted from "http://www.hjenglish.com/new/p171078/")

幸福的真谛

我有一位病人，他是一个成功的商人，告诉我，在他患癌症之前，凡事如果没有确定下来他就忧心忡忡。对他而言，幸福是"拥有小甜饼"。如果你拥有了小甜饼，一切都一帆风顺。如果你没有小甜饼，生活就一文不值。不幸的是，小甜饼总是不断变换着，有时它是金钱，是权力，是欲望。有时，它是一辆新车、一份数额最大的合同、或者一个享有声望的通讯地址。在他被诊断出患有前列腺癌的一年半之后，他坐在那里，悲天悯人地摇着头，说："长大以后，我好像就不知道怎样生活了。当我给我儿子一个小甜饼时，他心花怒放。如果我拿走甜饼或者是小甜饼碎了，他就闷闷不乐。不同的是，他只有两岁半，而我已经四十三岁了。我花了这么长的时间才明白小甜饼并不能使我长久感到幸福。从你拥有小甜饼的那一刻，它就开始破碎，或者你就开始担心它会破

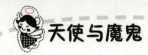

碎，抑或你开始担心别人拿走它。为了守护你的小甜饼，为了防止它破碎或者确定别人不会从你手中夺走它，你不得不放弃许多东西。你忙于不让自己失去它，甚至没有时间享受它。拥有小甜饼并不是生活的全部内容。"

我的病人笑着说癌症已经改变了他。不论他的生意是否一帆风顺，不论他在打高尔夫球时是输是赢，他有生以来第一次感到幸福。"两年前，癌症问我'什么重要？什么才真正的重要？'对，生命重要。生命。生命，无论如何你拥有生命，有小甜饼也罢，没有小甜饼也罢，幸福与小甜饼并非息息相关，而是与生命的存在有关。可是，时光一去不复返，谁又能让时光倒流呢？"他停顿了一下，若有所思，说："该死，我觉得生命就是那块小甜饼。"

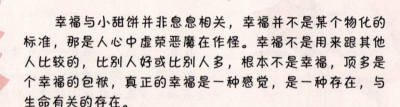

幸福与小甜饼并非息息相关，幸福并不是某个物化的标准，那是人心中虚荣恶魔在作怪。幸福不是用来跟其他人比较的，比别人好或比别人多，根本不是幸福，顶多是个幸福的包袱，真正的幸福是一种感觉，是一种存在，与生命有关的存在。

虚荣魔鬼篇
[之二]

Life Is a Cup of Coffee

Life is the coffee and the jobs, money and position in society, are the cups.

如果生活是咖啡，工作、财富和社会地位就是那些杯子。

Group of alumni (毕业生), highly established in their careers, got together to visit their old university professor. The conversation soon turned into complaints about stress in work and in life. Offering his guests coffee, the professor went to the kitchen and returned with a large pot of coffee and an assortment (一类) of cups—porcelain (瓷制的), plastic, glass, crystal, some plain looking, some expensive (精致的), some exquisite—telling them to help themselves to the coffee.

When all the students had a cup of coffee in hand, the professor said:

"If you noticed, all the nice looking expensive cups were taken up, leaving behind the plain and cheap ones. While it is normal for you to want only the best for yourselves, that is the source of your problems and stress."

"What all of you really wanted was coffee, not the cups, but you consciously (故意地) went for the best cups and were eyeing each other's cups."

"Now consider this: Life is the coffee and the jobs, money and position in society are the cups. They are just tools to hold and contain Life, and do not change the quality of Life. Sometimes, by concentrating only on the cups, we fail to enjoy the coffee God has provided. So, don't let the cups drive you ... enjoy the coffee instead." (214 words)

(Extracted from "http://news.163.com/09/0803/16/5FQ8R650000120GR.html")

177

生活是杯咖啡

一群毕业生，各自的事业都已有所成就，相约一起去看望他们的大学教授。谈话一会儿就变成了各自对工作、生活压力的抱怨。教授去厨房端来一大壶咖啡招待这些客人，拿出各式各样的咖啡杯——陶瓷的、塑料的、玻璃的、水晶的，有普通的、有价值不斐的、有做工精致的——让他们自己挑杯子倒咖啡。

当所有学生手中都拿了咖啡杯之后，教授说道：

"如果你们注意一下，就可以发现所有好看的、贵的杯子都被挑走了，剩下的只是那些普通的和便宜的。当然，每个人都想给自己挑到那个最好的，这很正常，但这也正是你们的问题和压力根源之所在。"

"其实你们真正想要的是咖啡，而不是杯子，但你们却都有意识地去挑选最好的杯子，并观察别人拿到的杯子。"

"现在想一想：如果生活是咖啡，工作、财富和社会地位就是那些杯子。它们只是维持生活的工具而已，并不改变生活质量。有时候，我们在过于关注杯子的同时却忘了去品味上帝赐予的咖啡。所以，不要成为杯子的奴隶……好好地享受并品味杯中的咖啡。"

人人都有虚荣心，那个虚荣恶魔从未离开，希望人生可以拨开繁琐与虚华，找到生活的真谛，工作、财富和社会地位不过是维持生活的工具，不要成为杯子的奴隶，好好地享受品味杯中的咖啡吧。

虚荣魔鬼篇

[之三]

Good Looks vs. Education

Your daughter should learn to work hard and look good at the same time.

你的女儿应该学会在努力学习的同时也把自己打扮得漂漂亮亮。

A curious mother ever asked, "My 15-year-old daughter is disinclined (不愿意的) to work for her GCSEs, saying her time is better spent preening (打扮) herself in preparation for assignations (约会) with her delightful, diligent, privately educated, moneyed boyfriend. She insists the money spent on nail-painting, hair-coloring and the like is an investment and will be more than repaid when he marries her. Is she deluding (使失望) herself?"

Here is the answer she got from an expert:

"Surprising as this may seem in the 21st century, your daughter's strategy is not unusual. Evidence on speed-dating gathered by the economists Michèle Belot and Marco Francesconi shows that women are attracted by rich men, while men focus more on a woman's physical appearance. Lena Edlund, another economist, has found that in the areas of her native Sweden where the wealthiest men live, women of prime marriageable age are over-represented.

However, your daughter is only 15; for Edlund, 'prime marriageable age' is 25-44. Your daughter is either going to have to get her hooks into

179

this chap unusually early, or she is going to have to keep him on the boil for another decade–a lot of nail–painting.

Not only is she concentrating her investments into a single asset by abandoning her education, but she may even be making her main goal harder to achieve. Belot and Francesconi have discovered that a strong social trend towards 'assortative (选型的) mating' means that although educated, high–achieving men are not interested in marrying a rich woman, they do like educated high–achieving women, rather than shallow girls with shiny nails.

Your daughter should learn to work hard and look good at the same time. Not only will it advance her immediate goals, it will also stand her in good stead (用处) for the rest of her life." (291 words)

(Extracted from "http://020.teambuy.com.cn/edu/info.php?infoID=31523")

美貌还是教育

一位好奇的母亲曾这样问道："我15岁的女儿不愿为拿到英国普通中等教育证书（GCSE）而努力学习，说是自己把时间花在穿着打扮上更有意义，为的是与她那个讨人喜欢、勤奋、上私立学校的有钱男友约会。她坚称，花在美甲和染发等方面的钱是一种投资，在男友迎娶自己时就会获得更多的回报。她会让自己失望吗？"

以下是她从专家那里得到的答案：

"尽管在二十一世纪这种情况可能会非常令人吃惊，但你女儿的策略并不少见。经济学家米谢勒·贝洛和马尔科·弗兰切斯科尼收集的有关闪电约会的证据表明，女性受到男性金钱的吸引，而男性更关注女性的容貌。另一位经济学家莱娜·埃德隆德发现，在她的国家瑞典——在最富有男士生活的地区，最佳适婚年龄的女性比例过高。

不过，你的女儿只有15岁；在埃德隆德看来，'最佳适婚年龄'是25岁至44岁。你的女儿要么必须及早把这家伙弄到手，要么就必须设法让他保持激情再等上10年——而这需要大量的美甲。

她放弃自身教育的结果是，不仅她的投资仅集中于单一的资产，而且可能会让她的主要目标更加难以实现。贝洛和弗兰切斯科尼发现，现在存在一种强烈的'选型婚配'社交趋势，即尽管受过教育的成功男士对与有钱女士结婚不感兴趣，但他们确实喜欢受过教育的成功女士，而不是指甲闪亮的浅薄女子。

你的女儿应该学会在努力学习的同时也把自己打扮得美丽动人。这不仅能帮她提前实现当前的目标，而且也会在以后的日子里让她受益无穷。"

这是一个内在和外在的话题，文中的女儿已经向虚荣恶魔投降了，也许某次"围猎"她猎到了"猎物"，但她绝对无法留住她的"猎物"，因为初次见面的表面文章无法做足一辈子，后续的气质和内涵是偶尔的虚华所无法打扮的。

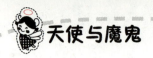

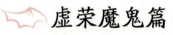

虚荣魔鬼篇
[之四]

A Lesson

> I hope you can understand that though you have a lot to learn, what you must learn first is to respect every person.
>
> 我希望你明白，虽然你要学习的东西很多，但你首先要学会尊重每一个人。

One day in the afternoon, in the garden of the famous Giant Elephant Group Headquarter Building located in Manhattan, New York, a gray-haired old man was concentrating on trimming (修剪) low shrubs (灌木).

All of a sudden, a mass of tissue was thrown from somewhere on the trimmed shrubs. The white tissue was especially dazzling (炫目) on the green shrubs. The old man looked up and saw a middle-aged woman sitting on a bench in the garden who threw the tissue. The woman kept groaning to her son while looking at the old man with great contempt. The old man did not say anything and picked up the tissue and put it into the garbage can.

At this moment, another mass of tissue flew over again. "Mum, what are you doing?" the boy asked with surprise. His mother waved at him, indicating him to keep silent. This time, the old man did not say anything again and picked up the tissue and then put it into the garbage can again. However, when the old man picked up the scissor again, a third tissue fell on the shrubs in front of him again. The same situation happened consecutively (连续不断地) and the old man picked up the tissues the woman threw for six times yet without showing any dissatisfaction or irritation (恼火).

"I hope you can understand that if you do not study hard, you will be as useless as the old gardener who can only do this humble job!" The woman pointed to the old man and educated her son.

Not until then did the old man realize the woman felt angry because her son did not study well and that she wanted her son to know the significance of studies by taking the old man as a live example.

At hearing what the woman said, the old man put down the scissor and walked to her, saying, "Madam, this is the private garden for Giant Elephant Group and only the staff can be admitted to be here."

The woman took out a document and shook it in front of the old man, saying with great arrogance, "I am a department manager in the company and working in this building!"

"May I borrow your mobile phone?" the old man said after thinking for a minute.

The woman handed her phone to him reluctantly (勉强地). The old man dialed a number and said several words simply. The woman, by taking this chance, educated her son again, "Look at this poor guy! He is so old now but still too poor to afford a phone. So you should work harder in the future!"

At this time, the woman suddenly saw the head of the HR department coming up hastily and smiling to the old man with great respect. The old man pointed at the woman and said, "Now I am proposing to sack this lady from our company!" "Yes, dear Mr. President! I will follow your order!" the head of HR department replied.

The old man walked to the boy and stroked (轻抚) his head gently, saying seriously, "Dear little boy, I hope you can understand that though you have a lot to learn, what you must learn first is to respect every person." (534 words)

(Extracted from "http://www.ebigear.com/news-124-72035.html")

教 诲

一天下午，在位于纽约曼哈顿的著名企业巨象集团总部大厦楼下的花园里，一位头发花白的老人正在聚精会神地修剪低矮的灌木。

突然，一团不知从哪来的卫生纸落在刚剪过的灌木上。白花花的卫生纸在青翠的灌木上特别显眼。老人抬头望去，看到一位中年妇女坐在花园边一张长椅上，是她扔过来的卫生纸。这个女人一边对身边的孩子说着什么，一边满不在乎地看着老人。老人什么也没说，捡起那团纸扔进了旁边的垃圾筒。

这时，一团纸又飞了过来。"妈妈，你要做什么？"儿子奇怪地问。他妈妈朝他摆了摆手，示意他不要出声。这次，老人仍然没说什么，走过去又将那团纸放进了垃圾筒。可是，老人刚拿起剪刀，第三团纸又落在了他面前的灌木上。如此这般，老人一连捡起了那个女人扔的六团纸，但他始终没有流露出不满和恼火的神色。

"我希望你明白，如果你现在不努力学习，将来只能跟这老花匠一样没出息，只能干低贱的工作！"中年女人指着老人在教育儿子。

这时，老人才明白，这个女人生气是因为孩子的学习成绩不好，她要让孩子明白学习的重要性，而自己成了她"现身说法"的"活教材"。

老人听到了中年女人的话，放下剪刀走过去说："夫人，这是巨象集团的私家花园，按规定只有集团员工才能进来。"

中年女人掏出一张证件朝老人晃了晃，趾高气扬地说："我是巨象集团的部门经理，就在这座大厦里工作！"

"我能借你的手机用一下吗？"老人想了一会儿说。

中年女人极不情愿地把手机递给老人。老人拨了一个号码，简单地说了几句话。中年女人又乘机教育儿子："你看这些穷人，这么大年纪了，连个手机也买不起。你今后千万要努力啊！”

这时，中年女人突然看到巨象集团人力资源部的负责人急匆匆地走过来，满脸堆笑地迎向老人。老人指着中年女人对来人说：“我现在提议免去这位女士在巨象集团的职务！”“是！总裁先生，我立刻按您的指示去办！”人力资源部负责人应声答道。

老人走到男孩面前，轻抚着他的头，认真地说：“亲爱的小朋友，我希望你明白，虽然你要学习的东西很多，但你必须要先学会尊重每一个人。”

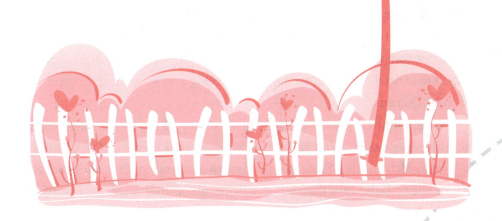

　　一个精美的心灵读本，让我们穿透虚荣看到本质。文中妈妈所有苦口婆心的教诲都因虚荣而变得苍白无力，而老人的忍耐与睿智却给了年轻人最好的言传身教，抛开虚表，学会做人，是最基本的教诲。

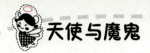

虚荣魔鬼篇

[之五]

The Tantrum

> Instead she found ways of punishment that left a more lasting memory than the short sting of a swat onour rumps.
>
> 她总能想出一些方法来惩罚我们，而这些方法远比巴掌打在我们屁股上更痛、更持久。

My mother was a vocal supporter of corporal (肉体的) punishment, but for all her talking she has never spanked (打屁股) my siblings, and me only once. Instead she found ways of punishment that left a more lasting memory than the short sting of a swat (拍打) on our rumps (屁股). One of the most memorable of these occasions occurred when I was four.

In the early 70s my mother attended college during the day while my sister was in school and I was in daycare. One day at daycare I watched an extremely tired mother attempt to pick up her daughter. The little girl asked, "Momma, are we going to McDonalds for dinner?" The mother replied, "Honey, not tonight. Momma has to run a few errands and then we have to go home and cook dinner for Daddy." "But I wanna go." "Susie, I said not tonight. Maybe, if you are a good girl we can go tomorrow." Susie immediately dropped to the floor, kicking and screaming, "I want to go to McDonalds."

No amount of pleading (借口) or scolding (责备) her mother tried stopped Susie's tantrum (发脾气). Finally her mother gave in, "Okay, Susie, let's go to McDonalds." Susie stopped yelling and smiling, then she grabbed her mother's hand and they left. I was delighted that anything I wanted could be had by throwing a tantrum.

186

That day my mother picked me up early from daycare because we were going to Sears & Roebuck to pay on a Christmas Layaway. I was excited by the lights and decorations, and as we walked through the toy section on the way to the Layaway Department, I saw a toy I had to have. It was a white and red telephone whose bells rang as it was pulled along on a string. Looking lovingly up at my mother I asked, "Mama, can I have that telephone?"

She replied, "Baby, not now, but if you are a good girl maybe Santa will bring it to you." "But Mama, I want that telephone right now." Her eyes narrowed and her hand tightened on mine. "Becky, you can't have that telephone today, but if you misbehave you can have a spanking."

By now we were standing in the long Holiday line in the Layaway Department, and I figured it was now or never. I lay down on the ground and began screaming, "I want that telephone," over and over again. Weary Christmas shoppers looked as my mother calmly said, "Becky, you'd better get up by the count of three or else. One...Two...Three."

Nothing. I was still in full tantrum. So then she lay down beside me on the floor, and began kicking and screaming, "I want a new car, I want a new house, I want some jewelry, I want..." Shocked, I stood up.

"Mama, stop. Mama get up," I tearfully pleaded.

She stood, and brushed herself off. At first stunned (吃惊), the others waiting in line began to sporadically (零星地) clap, and before I knew it they were cheering and laughing and patting my mother on her back. She blushed and took a little bow and the next thirty minutes in line was pure misery for me as various parents leaving the Layaway Department, shaking their heads at me and saying with a smile, "Your mom got you good. I bet you'll never try that again."

And I didn't, because it left a lasting mental picture more effective than any physical mark. (576 words)

187

发脾气

我妈妈说她支持体罚，但是只是说说。她就从来没有打过我的姐姐妹妹（只有一次打了我屁股）。她总能想出一些方法来惩罚我们，而这些方法远比巴掌打在我们屁股上更痛、更持久。我记得最清楚的一次发生在我四岁那年。

七十年代初期，妈妈白天去上大学，我姐姐当时还在念书，我则上了托儿所。有一天，我在托儿所里看到一位疲惫不堪的母亲来接她的女儿回家。只听那个小女孩问："妈妈，我们晚上去麦当劳，好吗？"那位母亲回答说："今晚不行，宝贝。妈妈还有事情要做，做完后还要回家给你爸爸做饭。""但是我想去嘛！""苏茜，今晚不行。你听话，妈妈明天带你去。" 小女孩听完马上就坐在地上，蹬着脚嚷了起来："我要去麦当劳，我要去麦当劳……"

不管那位母亲怎么好说歹说，苏茜还是不依。最后那位母亲让步了："好吧，我们去麦当劳。" 苏茜马上停止了哭喊，拉住妈妈的手高高兴兴地离开了。我很高兴，原来只要发发脾气就可以得到我想要的东西啦！

那一天我妈妈提前到了托儿所来接我，因为我们要去西尔斯商场拿我们预定的圣诞礼物。一路上，我被商场里花花绿绿的灯饰吸引住了。在路过玩具专卖区的时候，我一下子就看上了一件玩具，那是一个红白相间的电话机，只要拉一下上面的绳子就会发出动听的铃声。我抬头很乖巧地对妈妈说："妈妈，能买那个玩具电话机给我吗？"

妈妈回答说："宝宝，现在不行。如果你表现好的话，说不定圣诞老人会送你一个。""但我现在就想要嘛！""贝基，今天不能买那个电话机，如果你再胡闹的话我就要打你屁股了。" 妈妈皱起眉头握紧了我的手。

我们当时在定购部收银处，那里有很多人排起了长队。我觉得机不可失，不争取的话电话机就没指望了。我一屁股坐在地上尖叫了起来："我要电话机，我要电话机！"这么一嚷，周围购物的人们都回过头来。只听见我妈妈很平静地说："贝基，当我数到三的时候你最好站起来，一……二……三。"

我没有起来，还在继续大发脾气。这时妈妈也在我身边坐下，开始蹬着脚叫了起来："我想要部新车，我想要座新房子，还有珠宝，我还要……"我吓得马上站了起来。

"妈妈，不要这样，妈妈，你起来啊！"我泪眼汪汪地请求说。

妈妈站起来拍了拍衣服，愣住了的人群开始稀稀拉拉地鼓起掌来。我还没醒悟过来怎么回事，他们已经欢快地笑了起来，还不时地拍妈妈的肩膀表示鼓励。妈妈脸红红的，向大家鞠了个躬表示感谢。接下来半个小时的排队时间对我来说难熬极了。家长们在离开前都会冲我摇头，笑呵呵地说："你妈妈是为你好，我敢说你以后再也不会这样做了！"

我后来的确没有再这么做了，因为这实在太刻骨铭心了，那教训比打在身上的印记还更深刻。

小孩子心中的虚荣恶魔更为明显，要泼打滚耍脾气也许对实现目的更有效，但在他们还没有明白更多的事理之前，有很多事他们永远也不会明白。文中的妈妈做了跟孩子一样的举动之后，孩子才能真正意识到她行为的对错，也许这更能让她看到自己吧。